The BLACKBIRCH ENCYCLOPEDIA of Science & Invention

by Jenny Tesar and Bryan Bunch

VOLUME I
A–D

BLACKBIRCH PRESS, INC.

WOODBRIDGE, CONNECTICUT

How to Use These Books

The *Blackbirch Encyclopedia of Science & Invention* not only informs readers with entries on key developments, concepts, and people in science, it also presents a "snapshot" background and classification for each topic. To get the most from these books, readers may want to know the purpose of the infographic material that accompanies an entry.

The names and concepts following the idea light bulb 💡 list the people, theories, and discoveries that have contributed significantly to that entry's scientific development. Words or names that appear on the lists in **CAPITAL LETTERS** have a separate entry in the encyclopedia. Likewise, any words or names that appear in **boldface** in the text appear as separate entries in the encyclopedia.

The icons that precede the text of each entry classify it within the scientific world. Here are the fields to which each icon refers.

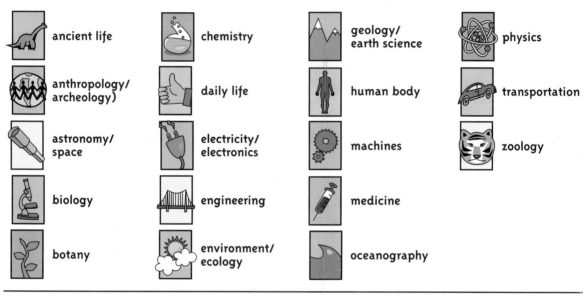

ancient life

chemistry

geology/ earth science

physics

anthropology/ archeology)

daily life

human body

transportation

astronomy/ space

electricity/ electronics

machines

zoology

biology

engineering

medicine

botany

environment/ ecology

oceanography

Published by Blackbirch Press, Inc.
260 Amity Road
Woodbridge, CT 06525
Web site: www.blackbirch.com
e-mail: staff@blackbirch.com

© 2001 Blackbirch Press, Inc.
First Edition

Printed in the United States.

10 9 8 7 6 5 4 3 2 1

Library of Congress Cataloging-in-Publication Data

Tesar, Jenny E.
     The Blackbirch encyclopedia of science and invention / by Jenny Tesar and Bryan Bunch
          p. cm. —
Includes index.
     ISBN 1-56711-575-6 (hardcover: alk. paper)
     1. Science—Encyclopedias, Juvenile. 2. Technology—Encyclopedias, Juvenile. [1. Science—Encyclopedias.
2. Technology—Encyclopedias.] I. Bunch, Bryan H. II. Title

Q121.T47 2001
503—dc21   2001001134

The Frontier of Discovery

Ever since the earliest humans, people have lived on the frontier of discovery. They have tried to understand their world and find ways to make their lives more comfortable. We do not know when or where people first tamed fire, shaped stone, or wove baskets. But each of these developments led to new discoveries, new ideas, new understandings, and new inventions, just as today's work on the frontiers of science and technology leads us to changes that only visionaries can anticipate.

Seldom is a discovery or an invention an end in itself. Scientists and inventors build incrementally on the work of those who came before, proving or disproving earlier theories, adding to or changing technologies. Each discovery raises new questions, each invention encourages creation of an improved model.

This step-by-step, fact-by-fact process is at the heart of science and technology. The principles that form the basis of this process are sometimes called the scientific method. First, people ask meaningful questions. Why is Earth's atmosphere getting warmer? How do fireflies produce light? Can materials be added to iron to help it resist corrosion? Where are new stars formed? How can a car engine be made more energy-efficient?

Once a question is formulated, an investigation begins. In 1930, John Gibbon wondered if a machine could temporarily perform the functions of the heart and lungs. He spent 23 years building and testing machines before creating one that could be used to keep a patient alive during a heart operation. During those 23 years, Gibbon had to answer numerous additional questions, such as: What happens to blood when it touches various metals? How can oxygen be added to the blood? How much oxygen does the blood use in a minute?

Often, scientists and inventors use the facts they already know to guess at a question's answer. Such a guess is called a hypothesis. Then they plan an experiment to test the hypothesis. Louis Pasteur hypothesized that fermentation is caused by microscopic organisms. His experiments showed that one-celled fungi called yeast ferment sugar, changing it into alcohol. And here's an important point: If an experiment's results are to be accepted, the experiment must be reproducible. That is, other people must be able to repeat the experiment and achieve the same results. (In science classes today, even children reproduce Pasteur's experiment!)

When enough facts support a hypothesis, a theory can be formalized: for example, all living things consist of cells, or the universe began with a big bang, or the earliest humans lived in Africa. If a scientific theory is not supported by facts, it will not survive. Many theories of the past have been discarded, including the beliefs that the Earth is the center of the universe, that atoms are the smallest possible particles of

People

… **of 50 years ago** did not have personal computers, compact disks, cell phones, or permanent press clothing. They did not know about sea-floor spreading, quasars, or the cloning of mammals.

… **of 100 years ago** did not have television, air conditioning, antibiotics, pop-up toasters, or spiral-bound notebooks. They did not know about DNA, the planet Pluto, or plate tectonics.

… **of 500 years ago** did not have photographs, electric power, bicycles, or thermometers. They did not know about bacteria, blood circulation, or moons around other planets.

… **of 1,000 years ago** did not have printed books, clocks, eyeglasses, or guns. They did not know about capillary action, the origin of fossils, or the causes of solar and lunar eclipses.

matter, or that flies and other creatures develop spontaneously from nonliving matter.

Similarly, an invention must be practical and relevant or it will be forgotten. Hero of Alexandria made a steam engine some 2,000 years ago, but because slave labor was plentiful the engine seemed unnecessary, and this innovation was considered merely an interesting toy. But when Thomas Newcomen built a steam engine in the 1700s, the invention was so timely that it changed the world. Among other things, Newcomen's engine helped to usher in the Industrial Revolution.

Though creative minds, hard work, and careful observations fuel advances in science and technology, sometimes a smidgen of luck helps, too. Paul Ehrlich spent years methodically testing hundreds of chemicals to find the few that would fight disease, but Alexander Fleming stumbled on penicillin by accident.

Investigation and observation are two of the cornerstones of science.

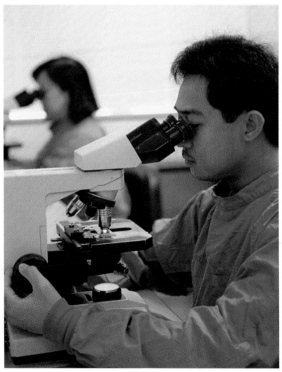

No one is infallible. The path to discovery has many dead ends branching off from it. Scientists who make great discoveries can also make big bloopers. For example, Aristotle firmly believed that all matter is composed of only four elements: water, earth, fire, and air. Antoine-Laurent Lavoisier was certain that acids were defined by oxygen content, when in fact hydrogen is the key element.

Often scientists—and society as a whole—cling to incorrect ideas from the past despite challenges by overwhelming bodies of evidence. Thus some major discoveries, rather than being met with cheers and honors, have initially encountered hostility and resistance. For daring to question ancient "truths" about anatomy and physiology, the "grandfather" of anatomy, Andreas Vesalius, lost his teaching position and Miguel Servetus [Spanish: 1511–1553] was burned at the stake. Geneticist Barbara McClintock's Nobel Prize-winning discoveries were ignored for years; ecologist Rachel Carson was demonized by the chemical industry for warning people about the harmful effects of pesticides on the environment.

Notable Quotables

If I have seen farther than others, it is because I stood on the shoulders of giants.

—**Isaac Newton**

The greatest tragedy of science is the slaying of a beautiful hypothesis by an ugly fact.

—**Thomas Henry Huxley**

All of us, at certain moments of our lives, need to take advice and to receive help from other people.

—**Alexis Carrel**

The scientist is a lover of truth for the very love of truth itself, wherever it may lead.

—**Luther Burbank**

The secret of science is to ask the right question.

—**Henry Tizard**

Merely looking at the sick is not observing.

—**Florence Nightingale**

The frontier of discovery is a messy place.

—**Neil de Grasse Tyson**

The science of today is the technology of tomorrow.

—**Edward Teller**

"The march of invention has clothed mankind with powers of which a century ago the boldest imagination could not have dreamt."

—**Henry George**

"Great discoveries and improvements invariably involved the cooperation of many minds. I may be given credit for having blazed the trail but when I look at the subsequent developments I feel the credit is due to others rather than to myself."

—**Alexander Graham Bell**

The interplay between science and technology is of immense importance. New inventions enable scientists to make new discoveries. The invention of telescopes led to the discovery of distant galaxies; microscopes led to the discovery of microorganisms; and balloons led to an understanding of the structure of Earth's atmosphere. New

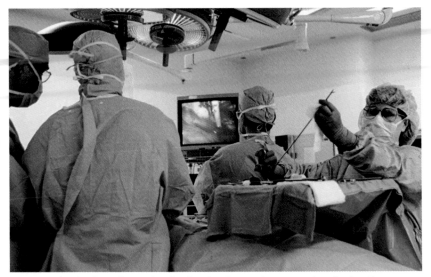

Science and technology often go hand in hand—advances in one area benefit the other.

inventions also enable scientists to take another look at "truths." A century ago, scientists theorized that the Moon's craters resulted from volcanic action. Today they theorize that the craters were formed when rocks and other debris from interplanetary space smashed into the Moon. The evidence for the modern theory is much more

Theories about space and the creation of the universe are constanly changing, as new equipment and technology enhance exploration.

convincing than that for the discarded theory, for it includes analysis of actual rocks and soil samples returned to Earth by astronauts and equipment that landed on the Moon.

Conversely, many scientific discoveries give birth to valuable technologies. The discovery of ultrasound and X rays led to medical tools; the observation that silver salts darken upon exposure to light led to photography; and Albert Einstein's study of the relation between electrons and light led to lasers. Not all scientific discoveries await technology, however, nor is all technology based on scientific understanding. Charles Darwin needed no new technology to propose his theory of evolution. Edward Jenner invented a smallpox vaccine before the cause of smallpox was discovered.

As the search for truth and understanding continue, new pioneers in science and technology will add their discoveries and inventions to those who came before, including the outstanding people whose work is described in this encyclopedia. ■

Acid Rain

When certain gases enter the atmosphere from factories, power stations, and certain vehicles, they react with water in the air. The main culprits are sulfur dioxide and nitrogen oxides, which react with water to produce sulfuric and nitric **acids**. The result is an increase in the acidity of rain, snow, and fog. The term "acid rain" to describe such precipitation was coined by Robert Angus Smith [Scottish: 1817–1884] in the mid-1800s. He observed how rain in England's industrial cities had become very acidic, and he linked the phenomenon to the burning of coal.

More than 100 years passed before acid rain was widely understood to be a serious environmental problem. In 1959, a Norwegian fishing inspector found fish populations were declining in lakes with mysteriously acid water. In the 1970s scientists reported that some lakes in the northern United States, Canada, and Scandinavia had become so acidic that they were "dead;" that is,

organisms could not survive there. Gases discharged from power plants were "fingerprinted" (chemically analyzed) and gases with the same fingerprints were detected

One cause of acid rain is gas emissions from factories and power plants.

hundreds of miles from their source. Such studies established that emissions originating from power plants in the American Midwest were tied to problems in northeastern lakes.

Methods to reduce acid rain and counteract its effects have been developed. For example, new technologies such as electric cars can reduce dependence on fossil fuels, and scrubber equipment—a type of **pollution control**—can be attached to smokestacks to remove acid gases before they enter the atmosphere.

RESOURCES

- Hocking, Colin, Jacqueline Barber, and Jan Coonrod. *Acid Rain.* Berkeley: University of California, Lawrence Hall of Science, 1999. (JUV/YA)

- Somerville, Richard C. *The Forgiving Air: Understanding Environmental Change.* Berkeley: University of California, 1996.

- ACID RAIN.

  http://www.iclei.org/efacts/acidrain.htm

Acids and Bases

DAVY (acid action based on hydrogen) ➤ **Brønstead** (proton), **Lowry** (proton)

Even before chemistry became a science, some substances were known as acids (sour) or bases (bitter) because of their taste. Mild acid is easily recognized in the taste of lemon juice (citric acid) and vinegar (acetic acid). Hydrochloric acid and nitric acid, discovered by alchemists about 1100, are chemicals powerful enough to dissolve metals. The most familiar base is lye, which was once used in soap but is strong enough to burn the skin. Acids and bases react with each other to form salts. For example, lye (sodi-

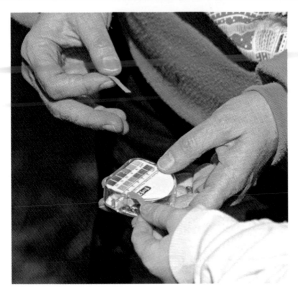

Litmus paper is one tool that is used to test whether a substance is an acid or a base.

um hydroxide) interacts with hydrochloric acid (hydrogen chloride) to produce table salt (sodium chloride) and also water.

In 1815, **Humphry Davy** concluded that acid action is based on hydrogen, but the true nature of acids and bases did not become clear until 1923, following the work of Johannes N. Brønstead [Danish: 1879–1947] and, independently, Thomas M. Lowry [English: 1874–1936]. Instead of hydrogen itself, Brønstead and Lowry focused on the hydrogen ion, or proton. An acid is a compound that yields a proton easily, while a base is one that takes a proton. The strength of an acid or base is related to how readily the proton transfer takes place.

RESOURCES

- Patten, J.M. *Acids and Bases.* Vero Beach, FL: Rourke, 1995. (JUV/YA)

- HISTORY AND THEORY OF ACIDS AND BASES.

  http://www.chemtutor.com/acid.htm

  http://www.chem.uidaho.edu/honors/acidbase.html

Addison, Thomas

Physician: helped found endocrinology
Born: April 1793, Long Benton, England
Died: June 29, 1860, Brighton, England

Historians often date the beginning of modern endocrinology—the study of endocrine glands and the hormones they secrete—to March 15, 1849. On that date,

FAMOUS FIRST

In 1829, Thomas Addison and John Morgan [English: 1797–1847] published the first book in English describing the effects of poisons on the human body.

Addison announced that a form of anemia was related to a fatal disease of the adrenals, a pair of endocrine glands that sit atop the kidneys. This was the first time that anyone demonstrated that the adrenals were necessary for life. (This anemia is now called pernicious anemia.)

In the following years, as Addison continued his studies, he discovered that the

FAMOUS FIRST

The first complete description of the microscopic structure of the adrenal glands was made by Rudolph Albert von Kölliker [Swiss: 1817–1905] in 1852. "I consider the cortical and medullary substances as physiologically distinct," he wrote. The fact that the cortex (outer portion) and medulla (inner portion) of the adrenal glands have different functions apparently was not realized by Addison.

fatal disease resulted from insufficient activity of the adrenals. He described this disease in 1855; it later was named Addison's disease by Armand Trousseau [French: 1801–1867].

President John F. Kennedy suffered with Addison's disease.

Addison also gave the first detailed description of appendicitis and made important contributions to our understanding of pneumonia, tuberculosis, and skin diseases.

RESOURCES

• ENDOCRINOLOGY: UNDERACTIVE ADRENAL GLANDS/ADDISON'S DISEASE.

   http://www.umm.edu/endocrin/addison.htm

Adhesives

Glue, paste, and cement are examples of adhesives (from the Latin for "to stick to"). Early glues were adhesives made from animal tissues, such as fish or mammal skin, animal bones, or milk. Most modern glues are forms of **plastic**—synthetic resins, such as epoxy— and are

Timeline of Adhesives

B.C.E.

3000	In Mesopotamia (now Iraq), asphalt is used to cement bricks together
	Egyptians use glue made from animal products
50	Romans use pine resins and beeswax as adhesives

C.E.

400	In Dark Ages, use of glue in Europe becomes unknown
1500	Home-made glue is once again used in Europe
1690	Glue factory opened in the Netherlands
1750	First British patents for animal-based glues issued
1808	First American glue factory opened
1850	Rubber cement is invented
1871	**Adolf von Baeyer** discovers the first thermosetting adhesive
1951	The powerful cyanoacrylate glue ("krazy glue" or "superglue") discovered
1958	Cyanoacrylate glues go on market
1974	"Weak" adhesives are introduced in Post-It notes by 3M

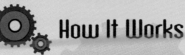

How It Works

Adhesives cling to surfaces partly from electrostatic reactions and sometimes from chemical bonds with surfaces, but most stickiness results from mechanical gripping. Soft adhesives penetrate small cracks and surround tiny bumps, then harden. Adhesives also create small bubbles that become near-vacuums when surfaces begin to be pulled apart. As a result, air pressure resists attempts to separate the surfaces.

soften with heat. Many glues and pastes harden when their liquid portion evaporates, but cement sets as water is added and combines with its powdered minerals.

RESOURCES

- Brief History of Adhesives.
  http://inventors.about.com/science/inventors/library/inventors/bladhesives.htm
- A Sticky Site (Make Your Own Glue, and More).
  http://www.thistothat.com

Agassiz, Jean Louis Rodolphe

Naturalist: showed effects of glaciers
Born: May 28, 1807, Motier, Switzerland
Died: December 14, 1873, Cambridge, Massachusetts

 In 1836, while climbing in the Swiss Alps, Agassiz became curious about glaciers. He began to study their movement and effects, concluding that the movement of glaciers plays an important role in carrying rocks and creating features on Earth's surface. Agassiz was the first to note that Earth had experienced at least one ice age, during which much of Europe had been covered with "great sheets of ice."

resistant to heat and chemicals. Pastes are adhesives made from starch, such as flour, and water. Cement is a form of **ceramic**, and is best known as the adhesive holding rocks and sand together in concrete. Rubber cement, however, is natural rubber dissolved in a material that quickly evaporates.

Adhesives are usually applied as liquids and harden, or set, after application, although some remain soft and pliable. Thermosetting glues are initially activated by warmth, but once set, will no longer

John Louis Rodolphe Agassiz

Agassiz also studied living and fossil fish. He used the principles of comparative anatomy—a new science founded by Georges Cuvier [French: 1769–1832] that involved looking at similarities and differences among species. Agassiz greatly increased knowledge of fossil animals and ancient seas.

In 1846, Agassiz visited the United States to lecture and study North American geology and natural history. He was an outstanding teacher, and became a professor at Harvard University. His vast collections formed the basis of the Museum of Comparative Zoology at Harvard—the first natural history museum in the United States.

RESOURCES

- Stephen Jay Gould, ed. *Finders, Keepers: Treasures & Oddities of Natural History Collectors from Peter the Great to Louis Agassiz.* New York: W.W. Norton, 1994.
- Louis Agassiz.

  http://www.ucmp.berkeley.edu/history/agassiz.html

Agricultural Revolution

Hunting/gathering ➤ **Israel/Jordan** (wheat), **Iran/Afghanistan** (goats/sheep), **Thailand** (chickens), **Mexico** (squash), **Peru** (potatoes)

Before the end of the last ice age, humans lived by hunting animals and gathering plants and slow animals, such as snails. But with a growing population of humans, food sources became scarce about 9000 B.C.E. Around this time, people all over the world discovered or developed new sources of food. People in Israel and Jordan started growing wheat. In Iran and Afghanistan herders kept goats and sheep for milk and meat. In Thailand, people used chickens for eggs and meat. In Mexico farmers grew squash and in Peru, potatoes. This world-wide change is called the Agricultural

People in Israel and Jordan were among the first to cultivate wheat.

Early peoples in what is now Thailand were among the first to raise chickens for eggs and meat.

Revolution. People continued to grow and improve plants and to breed and train animals, a process called domestication. By 1000 B.C.E., nearly all the plants and animals important in our daily lives today had been domesticated by humans.

See also farming.

FAMOUS FIRST

The dog was the first animal to live with—and aid—humans, at least 3,000 years before the Agricultural Revolution. The first known domesticated dogs were in Iraq, around 12,000 B.C.E., but dogs probably began to hunt with humans even earlier than that.

Air

VAN HELMONT (distinction of "air" types) ➤ BLACK (carbon dioxide), Rutherford (nitrogen) ➤ Ramsey (argon)

Early people knew that air existed—they felt the wind. The Greeks called air a basic element, along with Earth, water, and fire.

Nearly 2,000 years later, **Jan Baptist van Helmont** realized that there is more than one kind of "air." He invented the word *gas* to include air around us and "air from wood," caused by burning. In the 18th century, **Joseph Black** studied "air from wood," which he called "fixed air" and which we call carbon dioxide. Black made carbon dioxide by heating limestone and also found the gas in animals' breath. In 1772, Black asked Daniel Rutherford [Scottish: 1749–1819] to look for other gases in air. Rutherford discovered an unknown gas that, like carbon dioxide, would not support burning—nitrogen.

YEARBOOK: 1772

- Daniel Rutherford studies air.
- **Joseph Priestley** publishes instructions for using carbon dioxide to make seltzer water.
- **Antoine Lavoisier** shows that a diamond can be completely burned in air, turning from a solid into a gas (carbon dioxide).

The Earth's air is about 78% nitrogen and more than 20% oxygen, so nearly 2% is other gases. One small part (0.035%) is carbon dioxide. In 1894, **William Ramsey** identified argon as 1% of air. Neon and helium and traces of krypton, xenon, and hydrogen make up the rest.

See also atmosphere.

Air Conditioning

Cool air in caves and cellars ➤ Perkins (cool air up from tunnels) ➤ CARRIER (air conditioning)

From early times, people used cool air in caves and cellars as shelter from summer's heat. The first practical scheme to chill air inside buildings,

Air conditioners can be found in a variety of places, including cars, houses, offices and banks.

called air conditioning. Early air conditioners were installed in public buildings, such as theaters. In the 1940s and 1950s, room air conditioners, small units designed for one or two rooms, became popular. Soon all new American stores and many homes and cars were completely air conditioned. Warm deserts and tropical regions that had been sparsely populated became growth areas because of available cool air.

See also cold.

RESOURCES

- Cooper, Gail. *Air Conditioning America: Engineers and the Controlled Environment, 1900–1960.* Baltimore: Johns Hopkins, 1998.
- TIMELINE OF AIR-CONDITIONING PROGRESS.

  http://www.ari.org/consumer/history/timeline.html
- WILLIS CARRIER BIOGRAPHY.

  http://www.carrier.com/ghpnew/about/history.html

developed in the 1830s by Jacob Perkins [American: 1766–1849], used the same idea, bringing up cool air from tunnels.

In 1902, a different approach was developed by **Willis Carrier**. His method, which reduces humidity as well as temperature, is

How It Works

Warm air is chilled by **refrigeration**, with the heat removed from the air transported to the outside. Cool air cannot hold as much water vapor as warm air, so water condenses as the air cools; this liquid is also pumped outside. Fans push the chilled, dried air into the region that is to be cooled.

Airplanes

 DA VINCI (early concept) ➤ CAYLEY (glider) ➤ WRIGHT BROTHERS (motorized airplane), Blériot (aviator/airplane manufacturer) ➤ Britain (jet engines)

Insects, birds, and bats fly by moving wings up and down. In the 1400s, **Leonardo da Vinci** sketched machines that would flap birdlike wings, but he did not try to build them. Later,

FAMOUS FIRST

In 1927, Charles A. Lindbergh [American: 1902–1974] flew alone nonstop across the Atlantic Ocean from New York to Paris.

In 1927, Charles Lindbergh made the first trans-Atlantic flight in The Spirit of St. Louis.

people learned that machines with flapping wings are difficult to power and control.

In the early 1800s, **George Cayley** developed an easier way to fly. Cayley studied bird wings and recognized that their curved upper surfaces lift the bird as air flows over them. Cayley first built a small kite to test his idea. By 1808, he had invented the glider, essentially an airplane without an engine. In 1853, one of Cayley's gliders became the first heavier-than-air craft to lift a human for a sustained flight. In the 1890s, several efforts to use a steam engine to turn a propeller and lift a glider failed, partly because steam engines are heavy and partly because of the difficulty of controlling flight.

In 1903 the **Wright brothers** combined a lightweight gasoline engine with controls that enabled the craft to safely fly level and also turn at the pilot's order. Their flight on December 17, 1903, is considered the birthday of the airplane, although the first sustained flights took place five years later.

In 1908, a Wright plane flew for more than an hour, while the aviator Louis Blériot [French: 1872–1936], who had opened an airplane factory, advertised his product by flying across the English Channel. The first commercial flights were a cargo flight in England in 1911 and a short-lived passenger line in Florida in 1914.

There were two great spurts for aviation in the 20th century—World War I [1914–1918] and World War II [1939–1945]. The nations engaged in these wars introduced airplanes that could climb higher and were faster and more

Modern passenger planes can carry hundreds of passengers for thousands of miles without stopping.

Timeline of Aviation History

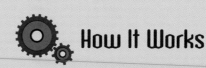

1492	Leonardo da Vinci conceives of birdlike aircraft
1589	First book to mention kites and kite flying in West (China had done so earlier)
1783	Balloon flight begins
1797	The propeller is used to power a steamboat for first known time
1799	George Cayley begins to design gliders
1842	W.S. Henson begins to design steam-powered gliders
1853	First glider flight to carry a human
1871	Otto Lilienthal [German: 1848–1896] begins to develop steerable gliders
1890	Clément Ader's *Eole* is first powered heavier-than-air craft to lift off ground, but immediately crashes
1895	Otto Lilienthal builds first glider to soar higher than its takeoff point
1895	Samuel Langley flies a steam-driven, pilotless airplane, although it crashes after a short flight (1.2 km)
1903	Wright brothers' first *Flyer* completes short controlled piloted flights
1915	Germans build the first all-metal airplane
1935	Lockheed introduces the DC-3
1939	The first jet engines fly, along with the first commercial flights across the Atlantic
1949	First test flight of the jet airliner Comet
1968	The Soviet Union introduces the first supersonic airliner, the TU-144
1970	The Boeing 747, the first jumbo jet, goes into service across the Atlantic
1976	The French-English supersonic jet the *Concorde* begins transatlantic service
1979	The *Gossamer Condor* becomes the first airplane to fly using human power alone
1990	The American SR-71 Blackbird spy plane sets a record of 1 hour, 8 minutes, and 17 seconds for a trip from California to Maryland

How It Works

Any airplane moves forward by pushing air behind it, whether a propeller or a jet engine moves the air. Forward motion produces lift in two ways. Upper surfaces of wings and the plane's body are curved. Air moving over curved surfaces travels farther and faster than air passing along the flat bottom surfaces. Moving air above the curved parts has lower pressure than air below the plane; the airplane rises. Furthermore, an airplane's wing tilts up at the front, so air flowing below the wings pushes them upward. Manipulating the flow of air by flaps in the wings or on the tail assembly is used to control the craft.

reliable; they also trained thousands of pilots and mechanics. After each war, civilian aviation built on these innovations and employed the workers. The period between the world wars brought airmail and flights across the oceans, with the DC-3, carrying 20 to 30 passengers, the most popular airliner. After World War II, airliners using jet engines instead of propellers—starting with the British Comet in 1952 and the American Boeing 707 in 1958—became

The Stealth bomber is one of the world's most high-tech aircraft.

the standard for long-distance flights. Airliners grew in capacity from carrying just over 100 passengers in 1958 to as many as 400 passengers by 1995.

RESOURCES

• Butterfield, Moira. *Airplanes* (Supreme Machines: The Stories Behind Technological Marvels). New York: Barrons Juveniles, 1999. (JUV/YA)

• Jefferis, David. *Flight: Fliers and Flying Machines.* New York: Franklin Watts, 1991. (JUV/YA)

• Rabinowitz, Harold. *Classic Airplanes: Pioneering Aircraft and the Visionaries Who Built Them.* New York: Metro, 1997.

• Winkowski, Fred. *100 Planes, 100 Years: The First Century of Aviation.* New York: Smithmark, 1998.

• HISTORY OF AIRPLANES.

    http://brill.acomp.usf.edu/qbannerm/history.html

Alloys

Copper ➤ Fusing copper and tin to make bronze ➤ Iron ➤ Iron alloys with carbon ➤ Modern alloys

A metallic substance formed by mixing metals or nonmetals into a metal is an alloy. Copper, the first metal used for tools and weapons, is soft. About 2500 B.C.E., after a few hundred years of working with copper, artisans learned that fusing copper and tin ores together using heat, also called smelting, produces the much harder alloy bronze. Bronze also has a lower melting point than copper, making it easier to smelt. Bronze tools and weapons quickly replaced copper. As a result, the time of early civilization is called the Bronze Age.

The Bronze Age lasted about 1,000 years, ending when an alloy with greater

Alloys have been used in coinmaking for thousands of years.

Alloys Timeline

B.C.E.

2500 Bronze replaces copper in early Middle Eastern civilizations

1200 Iron replaces bronze for weapons and tools

1000 Brass invented; possibly by Phoenicians, but some attribute it to Romans a thousand years after this date

700 Solder, an alloy of tin and lead that melts at very low temperatures, is introduced in Greece for joining metal objects

500 Pewter, an alloy of tin and often lead used for dishes, bowls, and small objects, is in use in China

300 Chinese invent cast iron, an alloy of iron and carbon with a lower melting point than earlier types of iron

Romans discover amalgam, originally an alloy of mercury and gold

C.E.

100 Romans are using brass and also pewter with a high lead content

1614 Small quantities of steel are made by heating iron with carbon

1700 Eighteenth century domestic items, especially dishes, candlesticks, and other small household objects, are usually made from pewter

1800 About this time a bright pewter known as Britannia comes into use

1839 A very smooth alloy (Babbitt metal—tin alloyed with copper and antimony) is developed for use in bearings

1856 The Bessemer process for making inexpensive steel, a high-carbon alloy of iron, is introduced

1883 A super-hard steel alloy made with manganese is the first of modern specialty alloys

1896 The temperature-stable alloy invar is developed

1911 Stainless steels, discovered accidentally in 1904, are recognized; several different types are developed soon after

1916 The first alloy with strong magnetic properties is an alloy of cobalt with tungsten steel; later alloys, such as alnico (aluminum, nickel-iron, cobalt-copper and possibly niobium or tantalum) are even more powerful magnets

1932 The first alloy that remembers a previous shape is developed from gold and cadmium; given a particular form originally, the metal can be bent into a different shape, but it returns to its original shape when heated; later shape-remembering alloys are used in space vehicles

strength and hardness replaced bronze. Although we don't usually think of iron as an alloy, useful forms of iron are all alloys of the element iron with carbon.

Today, most common metals are alloys of one kind or another. Modern bronze, copper alloyed with aluminum instead of tin, resists corrosion, making it important in ships. Brass, a shiny alloy of copper and zinc widely used by the Romans and in the Middle Ages, continues to be popular for its decorative value. Some alloys are useful because they are soft, melt at low temperatures, or are low density. Many modern alloys are valued for special electrical or magnetic properties.

Alvarez, Luis W.

Physicist and inventor: developed methods of detecting subatomic particles; proposed cause of extinction of dinosaurs
Born: June 13, 1911, San Francisco, California
Died: August 31, 1988, Berkeley, California

 During a 50-year career devoted primarily to designing, building, and operating large devices for accelerating and smashing subatomic particles, Alvarez also created significant inventions in optics, was active in the two main scientific efforts of World War II, and identified the likely cause of dinosaur extinction.

⟫⟫⟫⟫⟩⟨⟨⟨⟨⟨
NOBEL PRIZE 1968

Alvarez won the Nobel Prize in physics for his system of detecting subatomic particles, enabling him to discover various heavy "strange" particles whose interpretation has shaped modern physics.

Before World War II, Alvarez helped identify cosmic rays and forms of radioactive decay. His war assignment began with radar research at the Radiation Laboratory at the Massachusetts Institute of Technology, where he improved radar systems used to attack German submarines. He also developed the system used to land airplanes during zero visibility. Later Alvarez devised the trigger used in some early nuclear weapons.

In 1980, when his son Walter discovered a thin layer of clay marking the boundary between the age of the dinosaurs and recent times, Alvarez analyzed the material.

He found the clay unusually rich in iridium and proposed that the iridium derived from a large body striking Earth, which then caused a **mass extinction**. Evidence since then has supported this explanation.

🖥️📖 RESOURCES

- Alvarez, Luis W. Alvarez: *Adventures of a Physicist.* New York: Basic, 1987.
- Codye, Corinn. *Luis W. Alvarez.* Milwaukee: Raintree, 1990. (JUV/YA)
- MEMORIAL TRIBUTE TO ALVAREZ.
  http://www.fas.org/rlg/alvarez.htm

Ampère, André-Marie

Physicist: developed laws of electromagnetism
Born: January 22, 1775, Lyon, France
Died: June 10, 1836, Marseille, France

Ampère at various times was a professor of mathematics, chemistry, astronomy, and physics. Prior to 1820, his main contributions were in chemistry, although his independent and original chemical discoveries paralleled those of other scientists, who received the credit.

In 1820, scientists everywhere rushed to understand the implications of the discovery by **Hans Oersted** that electricity and

YEARBOOK: 1827

- Ampère publishes mathematical formulation of electromagnetism.
- John James Audubon [American: 1785–1951] begins publication of *Birds of America.*
- Georg Simon Ohm [German: 1789–1854] discovers law of electrical resistance.
- John Walker [English: 1771–1859] invents a match that lights when struck.

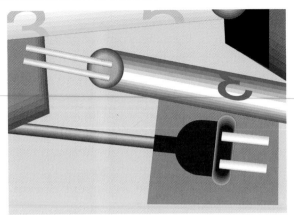

Units of electrical current are measured in amperes.

magnetism are related. Ampère began a series of experiments with electricity that led to the international unit of electric current being named the ampere. Ampère showed that wires carrying electric currents attract and repel each other. Current traveling through a coil becomes an electromagnet, with the amount of magnetism a measure of the size of the current. In 1827, he put these discoveries into mathematical form, known as Ampère's laws.

RESOURCES

- Dunsheath, Percy. *Giants of Electricity.* New York: Crowell, 1967.

Anatomy

ARISTOTLE (observation), **Herophilus** (brain), **Erasistratus** (nerves) ➤ **GALEN** (dissection) ➤ **VESALIUS** (internal organs), **Falloppio** (eye muscles, tear ducts, Fallopian tubes), **Eustachio** (tooth structure), **FABRICIUS** (valves in veins), **HARVEY** (blood circulation) ➤ **VAN LEEUWENHOEK** (muscle fibers), **MALPIGHI** (capillaries) ➤ **Buffon/Cuvier** (comparative anatomy), **BAER/Lankester** (developmental anatomy)

 The earliest written records of the study of anatomy (the structure of organisms) come from the ancient Greeks. **Aristotle** dissected plants and ani-

mals and emphasized the importance of direct observation. Herophilus [Greek: c. 335 B.C.E. –c. 280 B.C.E.] showed that the brain is the center of the human nervous system. Erasistratus [Greek: c. 310 B.C.E. –c. 250 B.C.E.] distinguished between sensory and motor nerves.

After the Roman Empire was founded in 27 B.C.E., human dissections were discouraged. The greatest physician of ancient Rome, **Claudius Galen**, based his understanding of human anatomy on his dissections of pigs and other animals. He made some valuable discoveries, but he

An example of a Vesalius anatomical illustration.

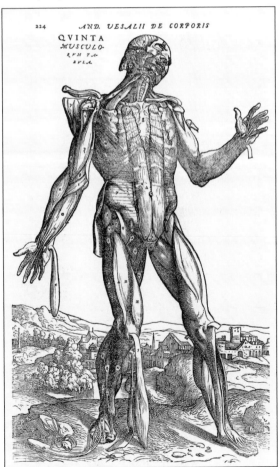

made many errors, too. He also accepted many false beliefs of the past, such as the belief that blood forms in the liver. Nonetheless, for the next 1,400 years, Galen's work was considered the absolute truth.

The Renaissance that began in Europe in the late 14th century was marked by renewed interest in learning. The modern study of anatomy began with **Andreas Vesalius** in the 16th century. Based on dissections, he accurately described the internal organs of the human body. Gabriele Falloppio [Italian: 1523–1562] described eye muscles, tear ducts, and tubes between the ovary and the uterus, known called Fallopian tubes. Bartolomeo

Eustachio [Italian: 1513–1574] described tooth structure and the tube that connects the middle ear to the back of the throat, now called the Eustachian tube.

Hieronymus Fabricius described the valves in veins. This led to the discovery by **William Harvey** of how the heart acts as a pump and how blood circulates through arteries and veins.

The invention of the compound **microscope** in the 17th century enabled **Antoni van Leeuwenhoek** to observe muscle fibers and **Marcello Malpighi** to discover blood capillaries; Malpighi also wrote the first descriptions of many insect and plant structures.

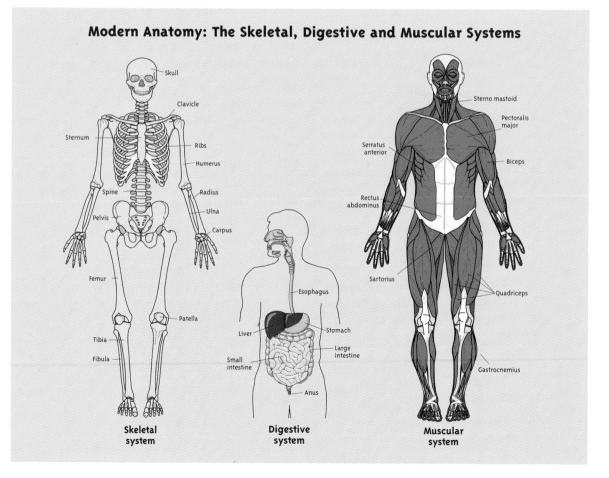

Modern Anatomy: The Skeletal, Digestive and Muscular Systems

Skeletal system — Skull, Clavicle, Sternum, Ribs, Humerus, Spine, Radius, Ulna, Pelvis, Carpus, Femur, Patella, Tibia, Fibula

Digestive system — Esophagus, Liver, Stomach, Large intestine, Small intestine, Anus

Muscular system — Sterno mastoid, Pectoralis major, Serratus anterior, Biceps, Rectus abdominus, Sartorius, Quadriceps, Gastrocnemius

Skeletal system

Digestive system

Muscular system

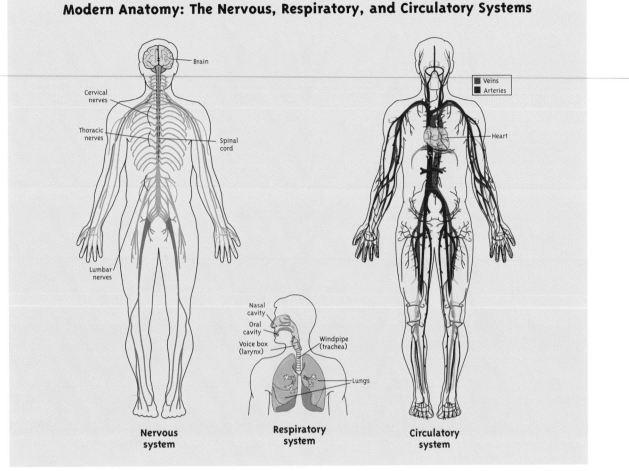

Modern Anatomy: The Nervous, Respiratory, and Circulatory Systems

Brain

Cervical
nerves

Thoracic
nerves

Spinal
cord

Lumbar
nerves

Veins
Arteries

Heart

Nasal
cavity

Oral
cavity

Voice box
(larynx)

Windpipe
(trachea)

Lungs

**Nervous
system**

**Respiratory
system**

**Circulatory
system**

As microscopes improved, anatomists could study ever-tinier structures. Microscopes led to the discovery that all organisms are composed of **cells**—and eventually to the discovery that the anatomy of cells varies tremendously from one body structure to another.

George Buffon [French: 1707–1788] and George Cuvier [French: 1769–1832] founded the science of comparative anatomy (the study of similarities and differences in the structure of various organisms). Other anatomists, including **Karl Ernst von Baer** and Edwin R. Lankester [English: 1847–1929], built the field of developmental anatomy (the study of structures at all stages of an organism's life, including the embryo).

Today, the study of anatomy is closely related to **physiology**—that is, scientists study how structure relates to function. In addition, the principles of chemistry and physics are important to understand.

RESOURCES

- Persaud, T.V. *A History of Anatomy: The Post-Vesalian Era.* Springfield, IL: Charles C. Thomas, 1997.
- Sawday, John. *The Body Emblazoned.* New York: Routledge, 1996.

Andrews, Roy Chapman

Naturalist: fossil hunter
Born: January 26, 1884, Beloit, Wisconsin
Died: March 11, 1960, Carmel, California

In 1920, Andrews asked his employer, the American Museum of Natural History in New York City, to fund the first scientific expedition to the Gobi Desert in Mongolia. Andrews hoped to find evidence of the origins of humans. In this, he was unsuccessful. But the Gobi expedition made numerous important discoveries, including the first dinosaur eggs ever identified (disproving the theory that dinosaurs gave birth to live young, as some scientists had believed). Many **fossils** of a large plant-eating dinosaur, Protoceratops, were found in the area and Andrews concluded that the eggs were Protoceratops eggs. On one nest of eggs was the skeleton of a small meat-eating dinosaur. Andrews believed this dinosaur died while trying to eat the eggs. He named it Oviraptor, or "egg hunter." It wasn't until the 1990s that scientists on another expedition from the museum proved that Oviraptor didn't deserve its bad reputation. The Oviraptor wasn't eating another dinosaur's eggs but protecting her own eggs!

Andrews spent his entire career at the American Museum of Natural History. He joined the staff in 1906 and rose to become the director from 1934 to 1941. During his career he traveled widely and helped make the museum's collection one of the finest in the world.

An Oviraptor protects her eggs against predatory dinosaurs.

 **RESOURCES**

• Bausum, Ann. *Dragon Bones and Dinosaur Eggs: A Photobiography of Explorer Roy Chapman Andrews.* Washington, DC: National Geographic, 2000. (JUV/YA)

• HISTORY IN THE DESERT.
http://www.amnh.org/science/expeditions/gobi/index.html

• ROY CHAPMAN ANDREWS
http://www.unmuseum.com/andrews.htm

Anesthetics

DAVY (nitrous oxide), **FARADAY** (ether), **Long** (anesthetized surgery), **Morton** (first public demonstration)

Even during ancient times, physicians searched for anesthetics—ways to dull the pain of surgery. Opium, alcohol, and mandrake root were given orally, but their effectiveness was limited. Often, doses were so large that the patient died—not from the operation but from the drugs.

In 1800, **Humphry Davy** noticed that inhaling nitrous oxide relieves pain—and provokes laughter. He called it "laughing gas" and suggested that it might be useful during surgery. In 1815, Davy's pupil **Michael Faraday** discovered that ether has a similar effect on pain.

The first use of a gas as an anesthetic during surgery occurred in 1842; Crawford Long [American: 1815–1878] painlessly removed a tumor from a patient's neck after the patient sniffed a towel dampened with ether. The first public demonstration of ether anesthesia, by William Thomas Green Morton [American: 1819–1868], took place before a group of surgeons in 1844.

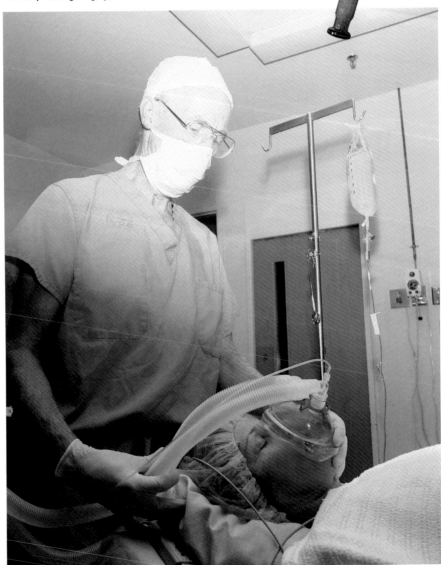

Modern medicine relies on inhaled anesthesia to put patients to sleep during surgery,

Nitrous oxide and ether continue to be used, but scientists have discovered many additional anesthetics including the widely used sodium thiopenthal, halothane, and trichlorethylene. Some anesthetics are administered by masks, as the patient breathes; others are given intravenously or applied to the skin to block sensation in a localized part of the body.

RESOURCES
- THE VIRTUAL MUSEUM OF ANESTHESIOLOGY.
  http://www.anesthesia-history.org/vma.htm
- ANESTHESIA HISTORY FILES.
  http://www.anes.uab.edu/aneshist/aneshist.htm

Animal Behavior

DARWIN (evolution) ➤ Whitman (instinct), Heinroth (imprinting), Pavlov (conditioning) ➤ Tinbergen, Lorenz, von Frisch, Wilson, Goodall, Schaller

People have always studied the behavior of animals. More than 40,000 years ago, people saw that some kinds of animals live in herds while others are solitary creatures. They noted that animals follow certain trails, use watering holes at dawn and dusk, or disappear during certain seasons of the year. Such knowledge helped people hunt and trap animals for food.

The scientific study of animal behavior began after **Charles Darwin** introduced the theory of **evolution** by natural selection in 1858. Scientists wondered what behaviors helped increase the chances of survival for an individual and its species. They also wanted to know why these behaviors were valuable, how they worked, and how they were related to **anatomy** and **physiology**.

One of the founding fathers of ethology—the science of animal behavior—was Charles O. Whitman [American: 1842–1910]. Around 1900, he studied the ritualized postures and movements that pigeons use in communicating with one another. He coined the term "instinct" to describe such behavior. About the same time, Oskar Heinroth [German: 1871–1945] studied ducks and discovered imprinting—behavior learned by very young animals in response to certain stimuli. **Ivan Pavlov**, working with dogs, discovered a learned behavior called conditioning.

The work of these pioneers was followed by that of many other outstanding scientists, including **Nikolaas Tinbergen, Konrad**

The construction method of a spider web can be predicted according to the species of spider.

Lorenz, Karl von Frisch, Edward O. Wilson, Jane Goodall, and **George Schaller**. Some studies are conducted in laboratories and are largely experimental. Other studies are primarily observational, involving watching what animals do in their natural habitats.

Understanding animal behavior has been important to human survival.

🖥📖 RESOURCES

- Hauser, Marc. Wild Minds: *What Animals Really Think*. New York: Henry Holt, 2000.
- Page, George. *Inside the Animal Mind*. Garden City, NY: Doubleday, 1999.
- Payne, Katy. *Silent Thunder: In the Presence of Elephants*. New York: Simon & Schuster, 1998.
- HISTORY AND PHILOSOPHY OF THE STUDY OF ANIMAL BEHAVIOR.
  http://www.biology.ucsc.edu/barrylab/ classes/animal_behavior/HISTORY.HTM
- INTRODUCTION TO ETHOLOGY.
  http://cas.bellarmine.edu/tietjen/Ethology/ introduction_to_ethology.htm

Anthropology

Blumenbach (early publication) ➤ **Boas** (cultural anthropology) ➤ **MEAD** (study of Samoans), **BENEDICT** (study of Native Americans)

The study of human beings includes physical anthropology, which is largely about anatomical differences between groups, and cultural anthropology, which deals with social interactions and traditions. Paleoanthropology, the study of very early humans and their close relatives, combines aspects of both. Anthropology has been systematically studied for about two centuries, beginning with an 1805 publication by Johann Friedrich Blumenbach [German: 1752–1840]. The accidental discovery of the first skeletons of Neanderthal humans in 1856 is the first event in paleoanthropology. Many believe that the publication in 1911 of the book *The Mind of Primitive Man* by Franz Boas [German-American: 1858–1942] initiated the beginning of cultural anthropology.

Native American

Anthropologists have struggled to understand differences between human populations. Their concept of "race" near the end of the 19th century embraced all

Native man, New Guinea

Kenyan woman

Bushman paintings, Zimbabwe

abandoned "race" as a scientific category.

Cultural anthropologists began by characterizing small populations. **Margaret Mead** analyzed Samoans in 1928 and **Ruth Benedict** studied Native Americans of the Southwest in 1934. Later in the 20th century, however, cultural anthropologists began to study much larger groups, looking for general theories of such ideas as "family" that might apply to all humans everywhere.

During the second half of the 19th century, paleoanthropology was not yet considered a science. The first Neanderthal skeletons were said by skeptical scientists to be modern humans deformed by disease. **Cave and rock art** was suspected of having been faked. By the early 20th century, however, evidence had accumulated that the earliest humans and their relatives had a culture that could be studied through their tools and other artifacts. Fossils of several different species of human ancestors and relatives were found in Asia in 1894 and in Africa beginning in 1924. More recently, paleoanthropologists have used studies of DNA to develop the theory that modern humans originated from African ancestors 100,000 to 200,000 years ago.

sorts of differences—for example, Italians, Irish, and Indians were thought to be different "races." By the early 20th century, anthropologists grouped humans into much larger divisions—Italians, Irish, and Indians were viewed as part of the "Caucasian race," for example. But when populations were studied with blood typing and **DNA** analysis, it became clear that the concept of "race" based on distinct differences among populations is not workable. Groups that differ in one characteristic, such as skin color or hair type, are alike in others, while superficially similar groups may have wide differences. By the end of the 20th century, anthropologists

RESOURCES

- Boyd, Robert and Joan Silk. *How Humans Evolved.* New York: W.W. Norton, 1997.
- Gallant, Roy A. *Early Humans.* Tarrytown, NY: Benchmark, 2000. (JUV/YA)
- Tattersall, Ian and Jeffrey H. Schwartz. *Extinct Humans.* Boulder, CO: Westview, 2000.
- Wilkinson, Phillip and Robert R. Ingpen. *A Celebration of Customs and Rituals of the World.* New York: Facts on File, 1996. (JUV/YA)
- MORE ABOUT ANTHROPOLOGY.
  http://www.anthro.net/

Antibiotics

ERLICH (Salvarsan) ➤ **FLEMING** (penicillin) ➤ **Dubos** (tyrothicin), **WAKSMAN** (streptomycin), **Duggar** (aureomycin)

Sometimes called "wonder drugs," antibiotics ("against life") are substances produced by microorganisms that kill or slow the growth of other microorganisms, particularly bacteria. They are used to treat a wide variety of infectious bacterial-based **diseases**. Important groundwork for their discovery was done by **Paul Ehrlich**, who spent years searching for a "magic bullet" to cure syphilis. He finally succeeded in 1910, with an arsenic compound he called Salvarsan. This compound proved that it was possible to use chemicals to kill disease-causing organisms without harming the patient.

Commercially produced antibiotics revolutionized medicine.

The first antibiotic to be discovered was penicillin, found by **Alexander Fleming** in 1928. However, it wasn't until the early 1940s that scientists recognized penicillin's great potential. Meanwhile, René Dubos

FAMOUS FIRST

The ability of antibiotic substances to inhibit bacterial growth was noted more than 50 years before the first discovery of such substances. In 1874, William Roberts [English: 1830–1899] observed that a *Penicillium* mold was unharmed by bacterial infection. Soon thereafter, Louis Pasteur and Jules François Joubert [French: 1834–1910] saw that anthrax bacteria could not grow in cultures that were contaminated with mold.

[French-American: 1901-1982] discovered tyrothricin, which became the first commercially produced antibiotic. In 1942, **Selman A. Waksman** coined the word "antibiotic." The following year, Waksman found streptomycin, which, unlike penicillin, is effective against tuberculosis bacteria. And in 1944, Benjamin Minge Duggar [American: 1872–1956] and coworkers discovered aureomycin, the first of the tetracyclines. Since then, some 5,000 antibiotics have been discovered, although only a small percentage have proved useful. Some are "broad-spectrum" drugs—

Timeline of Antibiotics

1929	Penicillin
1939	Tyrothricin
1943	Streptomycin
1944	Aureomycin
1947	Chloramphenicol
1948	Chlortetracycline
1953	Cephalosporin C
1956	Vancomycin
1962	Cephalothin

they are effective in treating a variety of diseases. Others attack a narrower range of germs.

Antibiotics revolutionized medical care. Deaths from tuberculosis and other infectious diseases dropped dramatically. In the 1950s and 1960s, this led some medical scientists to predict the end of infectious diseases. Beginning in the 1970s, however, the discovery of Lyme disease, toxic shock syndrome, and other previously unknown bacterial diseases made it clear that bacterial disease would not soon vanish. At the same time, "superbugs"—resistant to one or more antibiotics—were evolving. These microorganisms caused the antibiotics to lose some of their usefulness and necessitated the search for replacement drugs. It was also discovered that microorganisms can acquire genes for antiobiotic resistance from other organisms. For instance, it is common for DNA to be transferred between mating bacteria.

Doctors and scientists caution that antibiotics should be used sparingly and according to a prescribed regimen. Unfortunately, many patients want to take antibiotics for nearly every illness, even those caused by viruses, against which antibiotics are worthless.

RESOURCES

- Antibiotics: Past, Present, and Future.
  http://www.postgradmed.com/issues/1997/01_97/williams.htm
- Bacterial Resistance to Antibiotics.
  http://www.bact.wisc.edu/Bact330/lecturebactres
- In Praise of Antibiotics.
  http://www.asmusa.org/memonly/asmnews/may99/feature6.html

Antimatter

Dirac (electron theory) ➤ Anderson (particle in cosmic rays)

Science-fiction fans learn that when an antimatter creature encounters one of ordinary matter, both disappear in a flash of pure energy. Although there are no known antimatter life forms, **subatomic particles** of antimatter are common and a few **atoms** of antimatter have been created. These do vanish on

When matter and antimatter come together, they both disappear.

Matter-Antimatter Annihilation

encountering ordinary particles and atoms.

Antimatter was unsuspected in 1928 when Paul Adrien Maurice Dirac [English: 1902–1984] developed a mathematical theory of the electron. Dirac's equations indicate that the negatively charged electron has a positive twin. In 1932, Carl Anderson [American: 1905–1991] observed this "twin" particle in cosmic rays. As Dirac had predicted, a high-energy electromagnetic wave, or gamma ray, suddenly turned into an electron and its positive partner, which Anderson named the positron (also known as the antielectron). The transformation works the other way as well; when an electron and positron meet, they both vanish into a gamma-ray burst.

Dirac's equations apply to every subatomic particle, so each is accompanied by an antiparticle. An "antiproton" was first produced in a particle accelerator in 1955. The following year, the antineutron was seen. The neutron and its antiparticle are both neutral, but they spin in different directions and annihilate each other if they meet.

In 1995, scientists at CERN, a Swiss center for the study of particle physics, slowed antiprotons and positrons enough to allow formation of nine atoms of antihydrogen, the first anti-atoms.

RESOURCES

• Fraser, Gordon. *Antimatter, the Ultimate Mirror.* New York: Cambridge University, 2000.

• ANTIMATTER.
  http://livefromcern.web.cern.ch/livefromcern/antimatter/

• HOW ANTIMATTER FITS INTO PARTICLE PHYSICS.
  http://durpdg.dur.ac.uk/lbl/cpep/antimatter.html

Antiseptics

💡 **SEMMELWEIS** (lime chloride) ➤
LISTER (carbolic acid)

Antiseptics ("against decay") are substances applied to body surfaces to help protect against bacteria and other **disease**-causing microorganisms. Some 2,500 years ago, long before people knew of the existence of microorganisms, wine and vinegar were placed on battle wounds to try to prevent infection and decay. In the centuries that followed, many additional substances were tried, including some that killed not only the microorganisms but also the patients.

The modern field of antiseptics began in the mid-1800s. **Ignaz Semmelweis** greatly reduced illness among women in a hospital maternity ward by having doctors wash their hands in a solution of lime chloride before examinations. About the same time,

Topical antiseptics are widely used in modern medicine.

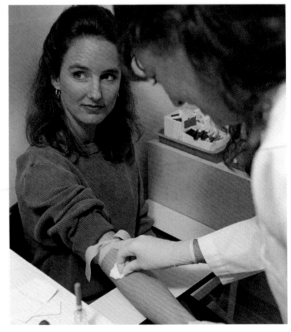

Joseph Lister began using carbolic acid in a similar way to limit infection during surgery.

Since then, scientists have learned much about the behavior of various antiseptics. For example, some antiseptics dissolve microorganisms while others disrupt metabolism, causing the cells to die of starvation. Hundreds of different antiseptic products are available, including soaps, mouthwashes, ointments, powders, and sprays. Many contain isopropyl alcohol or other alcohols—the most commonly used antiseptic substances. Iodine is another widely used antiseptic.

Appert, Nicholas

Candy maker, chef: invented canning
Born: November 17, 1749, Châlons-sur-Marne, France
Died: June 1, 1841, Massey, France

In 1795, the French government offered a prize to the person who could develop an effective method of food preservation. Appert's solution was to put food in bottles, like wine. He experimented with various techniques before reaching a conclusion: Food could be preserved if it was heated to boiling and sealed in airtight glass jars. In 1809, Emperor Napoleon Bonaparte—grateful to have a safe method of preserving food for troops in foreign lands—personally awarded Appert the prize of 12,000 francs.

FAMOUS FIRST
Initially, hammers and chisels were used to open cans. The can opener was invented in 1875. Tab can lids appeared in the 1950s.

British inventor Peter Durand decided that Appert's invention would be more practical if the container were metal rather than breakable glass. In 1810 he received a patent for creating a cylindrical canister made of iron coated with tin.

RESOURCES
- King, Irma B. *History of Canning.* Canton, SD: Tesseract Publications, 1988.
- A HISTORY OF PACKAGING.

  http://www.ag.ohio-state.edu/ohioline/cd-fact/0133.html
- HISTORY OF THE CAN.

  http://www.cancentral.com/history.htm

Aquaculture

China (practice begun) ➤ **Egypt** (fish in articficial ponds) ➤ **Europe** (fish in castle moats) ➤ **Pacific** (marine fish farming) ➤ Fertilizers/Hormones/Genetic engineering

Aquaculture, or water farming, is the raising of fish, shellfish, and seaweed under controlled conditions. The practice is believed to have begun in China around 2000 B.C.E. Ancient Egyptians raised fish in artificial ponds. During medieval times in Europe, people raised fish in castle moats.

Marine fish farming became prevalent in the Pacific around the 13th century. For example, Hawaiians would erect a wall around an area of shallow water, with slatted gates that allowed tides to flow in and out; small fish were carried into the area by the tides but once they grew large they were unable to escape.

In the United States, commercial fish farming began in the 1870s. The catfish industry began in the late 1950s in the

Modern-day aquaculture is a high-tech, big-business industry.

southeastern United States. Other products, including salmon, striped bass, shrimp, and lobster, followed.

At first, people simply confined organisms in ponds and pens, harvesting them when they had grown to a suitable size. Today, aquaculture is much more sophisticated. Fertilizers and high-protein foods are added to ponds. Hormones are given to improve growth rates and control reproductive cycles. **Genetic engineering** is used to develop fish that grow more muscle, are resistant to disease, and can survive in very cold waters.

📺📖 RESOURCES

- Stickney, Robert R. *Aquaculture of the United States, a Historical Survey.* New York: John Wiley, 1995.
- A BASIC OVERVIEW OF AQUACULTURE.
  http://ag.ansc.purdue.edu/aquanic/ publicat/state/il-in/as-457.htm

Aqueducts

💡 **Jordan and Syria** (first aqueducts) ➤ **Rome** (later aqueducts)

An aqueduct (Latin for "leading water") is a long channel that brings water from a remote source. Starting as early as 1000 B.C.E., aqueducts were built from rivers and springs to desert cities

⚙️ How It Works

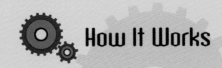

Aqueducts, modern as well as ancient, use gently sloped covered canals and tunnels to carry water from hills or mountains to lower-lying cities. When aqueducts cross valleys or streams, bridges or siphons carry the channel. In a siphon, the weight of water flowing down one side of a valley lifts the flow nearly as high on the far side. Modern aqueducts also use pumps to lift water uphill.

in Jordan and Syria. Other early aqueducts were built by pre-Incan civilizations in South America and by the Aztecs in Mexico.

Although Rome is built on the River Tiber, the Tiber became too polluted to use as a water supply. The aqueducts of Rome began with the Aqua Appia in 312 B.C.E. and by 226 C.E. there were 11 Roman aqueducts bringing at least 40 million gallons (150 million liters) of clean water a day to the city. Aqueducts built between 1837 and 1966 carry water from giant artificial lakes (reservoirs) to New York City. Very long aqueducts built from 1904 to 1991 bring river water from as far as 450 miles (725 km) away to the desert city of Los Angeles, California.

RESOURCES

•Aicher, Peter J. *Guide to the Aqueducts of Ancient Rome.* Wauconda, IL: Bolchazy-Carducci, 1995.
• Roman Aqueducts.

http://www.romagiubileo.it/guida/Pages/ eng/rantica/sAHy5.htm

Arches

Eygpt (small arches) ➤ **Rome** (architecture based on arches) ➤ **Europe** (pointed Gothic arches)

An arch consists of two pillars or columns connected by a curved top. Arches are usually made from heavy materials, such as stone, to keep the outward push of the curved part from toppling

Roman engineers built aqueducts and were the first to base architecture on arches.

Left: The highest section of a stone arch is held in place by the forces on its left and right.
Right: Eero Saarinen designed this famous steel arch in St. Louis, Missouri.

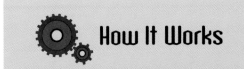

How It Works

When the curved top is a stone semicircle, the topmost stone, called the keystone, is held in place by equal but opposite pushes from the remainder of the halves of the semicircle. A pointed arch, called a Gothic arch, does not need a keystone, as both parts lean against each other. The side columns must be held in place by an inward-pushing force. Roman arches were often paired, so that the outward force from one balanced that from its neighbor. Gothic vaults are often supported by walls called flying buttresses that look like short wings added to the outside of a building, as on Notre Dame Cathedral in Paris.

the sides. Arches can carry great weight despite the open space beneath the curved part; they can be as strong as solid walls, yet they use much less material and thus seem more airy.

Small arches were occasionally built by ancient Egyptians, but Roman engineers were the first to base architecture on arches, often made of concrete. They also extended the sides of an arch to form a high ceiling, called a vault, and used a rotated 360° arch to make a dome. In the Middle Ages, Europeans built large churches based on pointed Gothic arches, sometimes using intersecting vaults. In modern times, arches are often used for bridges; rivers flow through the open arch, which also supports the roadway above.

See also cathedrals.

Archimedes

Physicist, mathematician, inventor: developed laws of buoyancy
Born: C. 287 B.C.E., Syracuse, Sicily
Died: C. 212 B.C.E., Syracuse, Sicily

 As a youth, Archimedes studied in Alexandria, Egypt, which was the foremost center of learning. While in Egypt, he invented the Archimedian screw.

YEARBOOK: 240 B.C.E

• Chinese astronomers observe Halley's comet.
• Eratosthenes calculates the size of the Earth.
• The Maya invent a place-value system for writing numbers.

Archimedes

This is a spiral in a tube. When the spiral is turned in the proper direction, it can raise water. This invention is still used to lift water from rivers today.

When Archimedes returned to Syracuse, he studied the mathematics of levers and wheels and showed how to use two or more pulleys to lift heavy weights with little effort. He claimed, "Give me a place to stand and I can move the whole world with a lever." The ruler of Syracuse, King Hiero II, challenged Archimedes to make good his boast. Archimedes used pulleys to launch singlehandedly one of the largest ships of that time, complete with crew aboard.

Hiero then gave Archimedes another great challenge. He asked the inventor to figure out whether the king's crown was pure gold. It is said that it was while bathing that Archimedes determined how to test the crown. Upon his realization, he supposedly ran naked though the city crying "Eureka!" [I have found it]. Archimedes had discovered that a body in fluid displaces an amount equal to the weight of the body. Using his idea—and his knowledge of the correct weight of gold—he proved that the crown was not pure gold.

Syracuse was attacked by the Romans in 212 B.C.E. Archimedes built levers that dropped boulders on the attackers' ships and he may have made other weapons. The Roman army managed to take Syracuse anyway. The Roman general told his soldiers to spare Archimedes, but one soldier found Archimedes studying a geometric figure drawn in the sand and killed him.

Aristotle

Aristotle

Biologist and philosopher: developed classification and embryology
Born: 384 B.C.E., Stagirus, Macedonia
Died: 322 B.C.E., Khalkis, Greece

Most of the many books Aristotle wrote are lost, but notes from classes at the school he founded in Athens—the Lyceum or Peripatetic School—were discovered by Roman soldiers about 80 B.C.E. and widely copied. These became the main source of scientific knowledge for the next 1,600 years.

Physicists think of Aristotle as a scientist who had mostly incorrect notions, such as the idea that heavier objects fall faster than light ones. Astronomers honor him for establishing the fact that Earth is a sphere, although his version of a universe with Earth at its center was disputed by

Copernicus and then **Galileo**. His greatest contributions were in biology, for which he developed a systematic classification of animals and conducted careful experiments in the development of a chick from an egg. Even in biology, where he was usually correct, his errors (such as stating that plants exhibit no sex or that the function of the brain is to cool the blood) were taken for centuries as fact. In other cases, however, Aristotle was far ahead of his time. For example, he was the first to recognize that dolphins are mammals, while sharks, even those that bear live young, are not. This correct conclusion was not generally accepted by biologists until the 19th century.

Aristotle's influence went far beyond science. As a philosopher, he established the laws of logic and discussed metaphysics, ethics, and politics. Aristotle even set forth literary guidelines that are still used by modern writers of plays and essays.

See also classification of life.

RESOURCES

• Parker, Steve. *Aristotle and Scientific Thought.* Broomall, PA: Chelsea House, 1995. (JUV/YA)

• ARISTOTLE'S BIOGRAPHY.

  http://www-groups.dcs.st-and.ac.uk/ history/Mathematicians/Aristotle.html

Arkwright, Richard

Inventor, cotton manufacturer: designed mechanical spinner
Born: December 23, 1732, Preston, England
Died: August 3, 1792, Cromford, England

In the early 1760s, **weaving** cotton cloth was a growing industry in England. Factories were unknown. Spinning cotton fibers into thread, then weaving the thread into cloth, was done by people in their homes. Arkwright heard about efforts to invent machines that could speed up the process, and undertook his own experiments. In 1769, he patented the spinning frame, a machine that spun fibers into strong threads of any desired thickness. The machine was too large to be operated

Richard Arkwright

by hand, so Arkwright built a mill powered by horses. Then, in 1771, he built a larger mill, driven by water power, and the machine became known as the water frame. In 1785, he switched to steam power.

By moving the manufacture of cloth out of homes and into mills, Arkwright helped to usher in the **Industrial Revolution**. He has sometimes been called "the father of the factory system."

RESOURCES

• RICHARD ARKWRIGHT.

  http://www.spartacus.schoolnet.co.uk/ IRarkwright.htm

• THE INDUSTRIAL REVOLUTION.

  http://www.eurohist.com/ the_industrial_revolution.htm

Armstrong, Edwin Howard

Electrical engineer: invented modern radio
Born: Dec. 18, 1890, New York, New York
Died: Feb. 1, 1954, New York, New York

Armstrong, who taught at Columbia University, invented frequency modulation (FM) as a static-free method of broadcasting in 1933, but no one wanted to try his new idea. AM (amplitude modulation) radio was the world's most popular entertainment medium, and commercial broadcasters were not interested in change. Armstrong persuaded Columbia University's Radio Club to use his invention for regular programs starting in 1941. Since then, FM has become the leading broadcast method for music and also television's sound system.

As early as 1912, while still a student himself, Armstrong invented an improved AM radio receiver and amplifier. A few years later he made the key invention that enables radio to be tuned easily to any frequency, the superheterodyne receiver. The original purpose of the superheterodyne, developed during World War I, was to lower the frequency of the electrical signals emitted by airplane engines so that the planes could be detected by radio.

RESOURCES

- Lewis, Thomas S.W. *Empire of the Air: The Men Who Made Radio.* New York: Edward Burlingame, 1991.
- BIOGRAPHIES OF ARMSTRONG.
  http://users.erols.com/oldradio/
  http://www.world.std.com/jlr/doom/
  armstrng.htm
  http://www.cinemedia.com.au/
  SFCV-RMIT-Annex/rnaughton/
  ARMSTRONG_BIO.html

Artificial Limbs and Organs

Paré (hand), GLUCK (hip joint) ➤ development of plastic resins, 3-D computer modeling

The earliest artificial body parts, in places such as ancient Egypt and Greece, were simple crutches, peg legs, and limbs made of fiber. It wasn't until the Renaissance in Europe that significant improvements began to be made. For example, Ambroise Paré [French: 1510–1590] invented a hand with springs. In the

Artificial Organs Timeline

1873	First artificial larynx implanted
1891	First hip replacement
1929	Temporary cardiac pacemaker developed
1938	Artificial joints made of stainless steel introduced
1942	First artificial larynx powered by electricity introduced
1943	Artificial kidney first used on humans
1943	Discovery of Dextran, a blood substitute
1949	First tests of artificial eye lens
1952	Artificial valve implanted in a patient's aorta
1953	Heart-lung machine first used on a human
1957	First portable pacemaker
1957	First artificial heart implanted in a dog
1958	First implantable pacemaker developed
1969	First artificial heart implanted in a human
1970	Development of total knee replacement
1981	Artificial skin introduced
1991	Artificial pancreas successfully tested in dogs
1998	Artificial blood vessels successfully tested in dogs

centuries that followed, artificial limbs were introduced that could be moved at joints. They worked with a complicated system of harnesses and straps. Then, in the second half of the 20th century—following development of technologies such as plastic resins and three-dimensional computer modeling—sophisticated limbs became available.

The concept of artificial skin dates back to the 17th century, when lizard skin was applied to wounds. Further experimentation with animal skins and human cadaver

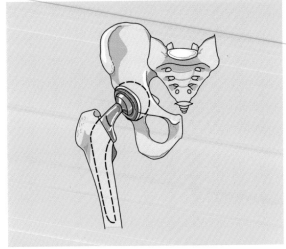

Human hip joint showing placement of inplant.

skin were somewhat successful in temporarily covering and protecting wounded areas. The first artificial skin, containing no living components, was introduced in 1981.

The first artificial joint was probably the ivory ball and socket cemented onto a hip joint by German surgeon Theodore Gluck in 1891. Stainless steel was introduced to the field in 1938. Today, titanium, aluminum, plastics, and other materials are also used, and a variety of joints, including elbows and knees, can be replaced.

Some devices that perform the functions of internal organs are external, including kidney dialysis and heart-lung machines. Others, such as pacemakers that regulate

YEARBOOK: 1953

- **John Gibbon** uses his heart-lung machine on a human for the first time.
- **James D. Watson** and **Francis Crick** discover the structure of **DNA**.
- Radial-ply **tires** are introduced.
- **Charles H. Townes** develops the maser.

heartbeat, can be implanted in the body. *See also* organ transplants.

RESOURCES

- PROSTHETIC HISTORY.
  http://www.nupoc.nwu.edu/prosHistory.html

Artifical Satellite

Kepler (moon satellites), **Newton** (orbit) ➤
Tsiolkovskii (artificial satellite) ➤ rocket propelled satellite developed

Originally, a "satellite" was a person who attended a member of royalty. In the 17th century **Johannes**

Timeline of Satellites

1957	First artificial satellite launched
1960	First weather, communications, navigation, and spy satellites
1962	The American *Orbiting Solar Observatory* develops first space telescope
1963	*Syncom*, the first communications satellite goes into geosynchronous orbit
1970	*Uhuru*, first X-ray telescope
1971	*Mariner* 9 orbits Mars
1972	*Landsat 1* is first Earth-resources satellite
1978	*Pioneer 12* is first satellite to orbit Venus
1983	*Infrared Astronomical Satellite* (IRAS) first infrared telescope in space
1989	*Galileo* launched; begins to orbit Jupiter in 1995
	Cosmic Background Explorer (COBE) launched—studies Big Bang
1990	*Hubble Space Telescope* launched
1996	*Near Earth Asteroid Rendezvous* (NEAR; now NEAR Shoemaker) launched; enters orbit about asteroid Eros in 2000
1997	*Cassini-Huygens* launched; scheduled to begin orbiting Saturn in 2004

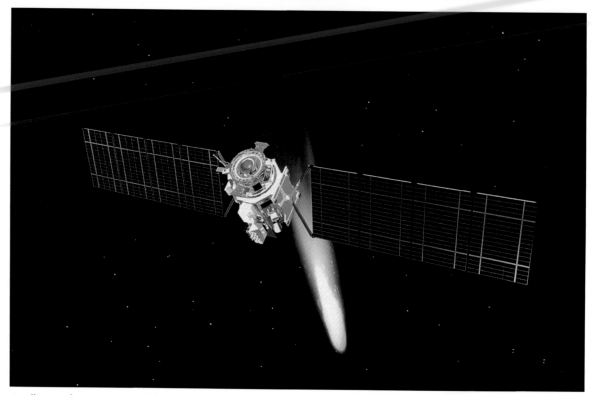

Satellites perform many critical functions from space—including the transmission of telephone and television signals as well as weather and navigation data.

Kepler called the newly discovered moons that travel around planets "satellites." Today, a satellite is any body that travels around (orbits) another in space.

The first person to understand how a body orbits Earth was **Isaac Newton**. In 1687, Newton described how a ball fired from a powerful cannon could, in the absence of an atmosphere, be put into Earth's orbit. Newton's idea was correct, but the technology needed for an artificial Earth satellite was not available. In the 1880s, Konstantin Tsiolkovskii [Russian: 1857–1935] studied the problem. He proposed that rockets propelled with liquid fuels could loft a satellite into Earth's orbit. In the 1930s, scientists in the United States and Germany developed such rockets.

After World War II, when German rockets were used as weapons, scientists felt ready to attempt an artificial satellite. American and Russian groups announced launches as part of an international project. The Russians succeeded first, launching the *Sputnik 1* on October 4, 1957.

Few recognized at first how useful satellites could be. In 1960, however, the earliest satellites for observing weather, aiding navigation, facilitating communication, and spying were placed in orbit. Today we rely almost completely on satellites for weather forecasting; for guiding airplanes, ships, and some cars; and for carrying television and telephone signals. Since 1962, space-based telescopes have become essential tools of astronomy. Other satellites, starting in 1972, inventory Earth's resources.

The first satellites traveled in orbits a few hundred miles above Earth, passing around the planet in about 90 minutes. Many of the most useful satellites of today are geosynchronous—they travel about 22,000 miles (35,000 km) above the equator, orbiting once in 24 hours so that they remain above the same location on Earth.

Although most artificial satellites orbit Earth, scientists have also put satellites in orbits around other planets, the Moon, and asteroids.

See also infrared radiation, space probes, space telescopes.

RESOURCES

- Gavaghan, Helen. *Something New under the Sun: Satellites and the Beginning of the Space Age.* New York: Copernicus, 1998.
- Parker, Steve. *Satellites.* Austin, TX: Raintree/Steck-Vaughn, 1997. (JUV/YA)
- A NASA SITE FOR SCIENCE SATELLITES (AND OTHER SPACE MISSIONS).
  http://spacescience.nasa.gov/missions/index.htm
- JAPAN'S SPACE ENCYCLOPEDIA ON-LINE.
  http://spaceboy.nasda.go.jp/note/Eisei/E/Eis_e.html

Aspirin

Willow bark identified as fever cure ➤ **Hoffmann** (derives acetylsalicylate)

Because willow trees grow near water and people once associated dampness with fever, willow bark was recommended as a cure for fever as early as 1763 (in a report to England's Royal Society, a scientific organization). Starting in 1838, chemists derived several forms of

the active ingredient in willow bark, but these harsh chemicals were too dangerous. In 1893, the German chemist Felix Hoffmann [German: 1868–1946], found a new derivative, acetylsalicylate, while seeking treatment for his father's arthritis. For most people acetylsalicylate safely reduces pain and lowers fever. Hoffmann worked for the Bayer pharmaceutical company, which named the new drug "aspirin" and began selling it in 1899.

Like earlier medicines based on the chemicals in willow, aspirin can irritate the stomach. Physicians also discovered that aspirin reduces blood clotting. Today, some people take small amounts of aspirin daily to prevent blood clots that can cause heart attack or stroke. Aspirin also prevents some damage from heart attacks.

YEARBOOK: 1899

- Aspirin goes on sale.
- An **automobile** travels faster than 100 miles per hour for the first time.
- First **radio signals** are sent by **Guglielmo Marconi** from England to France.
- **J.J. Thomson** proves that electrons are parts of atoms.

Assembly Line

Italy (early assembly line) ➤ **Evans** (conveyor belts) ➤ **FORD** (assembly line) ➤ robotic assembly

An assembly line consists of a single worker or small team of workers carrying out one step of a manufacturing process repeatedly. One team passes a partly finished object along to the next worker or team for the next step. The assembly line produces products faster than other methods. According to a report from 1436, a Venetian ship-builder could make ten galleys (a type of sailing vessel) in six hours this way. In 1784, Oliver Evans [American: 1755–1819] had the idea to move grain through a flour mill on a series of conveyor belts. These two ideas were combined in 1913 by Henry Ford [American: 1863–1947]. Instead of having one worker assemble one auto part, he moved the part along a conveyor belt while several workers in turn put it together, cutting assembly time by more than two-thirds. This success prompted Ford to use the same technique for entire automobiles, cutting assembly time from 12.5 hours to 1.5 hours per car.

Although the assembly line speeds up manufacture and reduces cost, it does have some negative effects. Endless repetition is boring and often causes worker dissatisfaction and lack of concentration. Errors due to inattention are also multiplied by the repetition. Such repetition can also be physically harmful to a worker. In recent years, repetitive tasks have often been taken over by **robots** while human workers monitor quality or engage in less automated tasks.

See also automation.

The assembly line introduced for automobiles is now used in all kinds of industries, modernized with the addition of computers and robots.

Asteroids

 Piazzi (discovery) ➤ **Herschel** (terminology) ➤ space probes take images of asteroids

Giuseppe Piazzi [Italian: 1749–1826], on January 1, 1801, observed a point of light moving across the sky like a planet. Piazzi named the apparent tiny planet Ceres, after a Greek goddess. **William Herschel** proposed calling Ceres an asteroid ("starlike object") because it looks like a star in a telescope—a point of light instead of a disk. Today, small rocky bodies that orbit the Sun are still called asteroids, although many astronomers prefer the name "minor planets."

Piazzi was looking for a new planet in the wide gap between Mars and Jupiter. Like Ceres, most asteroids are in this "asteroid belt"—millions of them. Ceres, 567 miles (913 km) across, is the largest asteroid in the belt.

Other asteroids—more than a thousand—have orbits much closer to Earth. Apollo asteroids are those that cross Earth's orbit. Scientists believe that Apollo asteroids sometimes hit Earth, causing great destruction.

Since 1991, space probes have flown by asteroids. Images reveal them to be large, misshapen rocks or perhaps piles of gravel. Asteroid Ida was found in 1993 to have a small satellite orbiting it. In 2000, the space probe NEAR Shoemaker entered orbit about the asteroid Eros.

RESOURCES

- Bonar, Samantha. *Asteroids.* New York: Franklin Watts, 2000. (JUV/YA)
- Peebles, Curtis. *Asteroids: A History.* Washington, DC: Smithsonian Institution, 2000.
- SKY AND TELESCOPE MAGAZINE.

  http://www.skypub.com/sights/asteroids/asteroids.shtml
- STUDENTS FOR THE EXPLORATION AND DEVELOPMENT OF SPACE (SEDS).

  http://www.seds.org/nineplanets/nineplanets/asteroids.html
- U.S. NATIONAL AIR AND SPACE MUSEUM.

  http://www.nasm.edu/ceps/etp/asteroids/

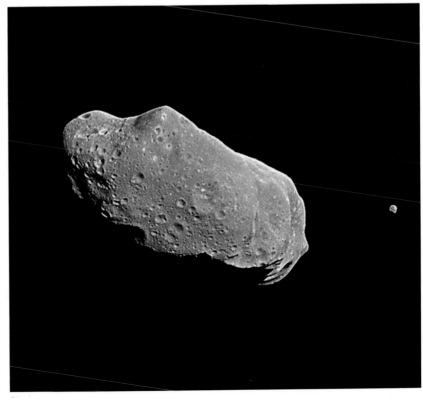

Most asteroids are large, misshapen rocks or piles of gravel.

Atmosphere

TORICELLI (barometer), **PASCAL** (atomosphere/ altitude relationship) ➤ **Teisserence de Bort** (altitude/temperature relationship), **Kennelly/Heaviside** (radio waves/ionosphere)

The atmosphere is the body of gases that make up the air surrounding Earth. The atmosphere thins gradually into empty, airless space. People once assumed that air pervades the entire

universe. When **Evangelista Torricelli** invented the barometer in 1643, he posited that it measured the weight of a finite column of air, also known as atmospheric pressure. In 1648, **Blaise Pascal** had a barometer carried up a mountain to prove that atmospheric pressure differs with altitude; at a higher altitude, a barometer gives a lower reading because there is less air above it. At the tops of high moun-

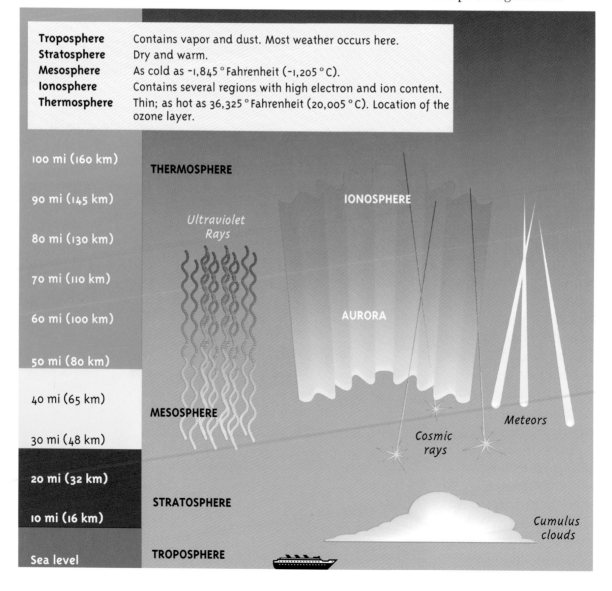

Troposphere	Contains vapor and dust. Most weather occurs here.
Stratosphere	Dry and warm.
Mesosphere	As cold as -1,845° Fahrenheit (-1,205°C).
Ionosphere	Contains several regions with high electron and ion content.
Thermosphere	Thin; as hot as 36,325° Fahrenheit (20,005°C). Location of the ozone layer.

100 mi (160 km) — THERMOSPHERE
90 mi (145 km) — IONOSPHERE
80 mi (130 km) — Ultraviolet Rays
70 mi (110 km)
60 mi (100 km) — AURORA
50 mi (80 km)
40 mi (65 km)
30 mi (48 km) — MESOSPHERE — Cosmic rays — Meteors
20 mi (32 km)
10 mi (16 km) — STRATOSPHERE
Sea level — TROPOSPHERE — Cumulus clouds

tains, air pressure is very low, as is the temperature, which is why high mountains have snowcaps even in summer.

In 1902, Léon-Philippe Teisserenc de Bort [French: 1855–1913], explored the lower atmosphere with kites and balloons. He discovered that, above a height of about seven miles (11 km), air temperatures rise. He later named the atmosphere's lower level the troposphere and the higher one the stratosphere. Also in 1902, Arthur Kennelly [British-American: 1861–1939] and Oliver Heaviside [English: 1850–1925] independently proposed that radio waves bounce back toward Earth from an electrified layer, now called the ionosphere. The ionosphere is above the stratosphere starting at about 30 miles (50 km) high.

The upper atmosphere is bombarded with energy from the Sun, which knocks electrons out of atoms to produce the ionosphere. In the stratosphere, solar energy creates a form of oxygen called ozone. Ozone absorbs the Sun's most destructive ultraviolet radiation and prevents it from reaching Earth.

The atmosphere differs on other planets. Mercury has almost none, for example, but that of Venus is very dense.

See also global warming, pollution controls.

RESOURCES

- Rauzon, Mark J. *The Sky's the Limit: All about the Atmosphere.* Brookfield, CT: Millbrook Press, 1999. (JUV/YA)
- ANNENBERG/CORPORATION FOR PUBLIC BROADCASTING COLLECTION.
  http://www.learner.org/exhibits/weather/atmosphere.html
- JET PROPULSION LABORATORY AT NASA.
  http://www.jpl.nasa.gov/earth/atmo/

Atomic Clocks

Atomic clocks measure **time** by counting the vibrations of atoms or molecules. These are motions that are constant for any particular substance. The concept was introduced by Isidor Rabi [American: 1898–1988] in 1945, and the first atomic clock was built in 1949. Atomic clocks are much more accurate than other measures of time (such as those based on pendulums or vibrations of a quartz crystal). One atomic clock, built in 1999 by the U.S. National Institute of Standards and Technology, would gain or lose less than a second if it ran for 20 million years.

The atomic clock is today's fundamental tool of measurement. Since 1967, the official length of one second has been 9,192,631,770 atomic "beats" of the form of the metal cesium that has 133 protons and neutrons per atom. This second is then used to define a unit of length, the meter; by definition, in one second light travels in a vacuum exactly 299,792,458 meters. Occasionally the length of a year must be adjusted by one second so that time based on the movements of the Sun and stars matches the official time measured by atoms.

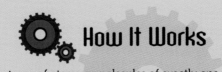 **How It Works**

A gas of atoms or molecules of exactly one type is fed into a resonator, which responds to a particular frequency (just as a tuning fork responds to a single pitch) and amplifies its energy. The amplified wave is measured to establish the length of a second.

RESOURCES

• Barnett, Jo Ellen. *Time's Pendulum: From Sundials to Atomic Clocks, the Fascinating History of Timekeeping and How Our Discoveries Changed the World.* San Diego: Harcourt, Brace, 1999.
• Landes, David S. *Revolution in Time: Clocks and the Making of the Modern World.* Cambridge, MA: Harvard University, 2000.
• MARSHALL BRAIN'S "HOW STUFF WORKS."
  http://www.howstuffworks.com/question40.htm

Atoms

Democritus (matter consists of particles) ➤ DALTON (matter consists of atoms) ➤ THOMSON (electrons) ➤ BOHR (atom concept)

The idea that all matter is made of small, indivisible particles is credited to the philosopher Democritus [Greek: c. 460–370 B.C.E.], who reasoned that fluids are formed from small round bits that roll over each other, while solids consist of tiny jagged particles that lock together. He thought the space between the particles would be empty—a vacuum. The influential **Aristotle** objected to the vacuum, while other philosophers argued that matter should be divisible even to the smallest amount imaginable. A few later philosophers followed Democritus, but most did not. No one thought that experiments could settle the question.

In the 17th century, the science of chemistry began to develop. By the end of the 18th century, chemists had discovered that compounds—such as water, salt, or ammonia—are always formed with the same elements in exactly the same ratio. In 1803, **John Dalton** concluded that these ratios occur because matter is made from atoms, with each element having atoms of a particular mass, volume, and chemical properties. Other 19th-century chemists showed that Dalton's idea explains how materials behave.

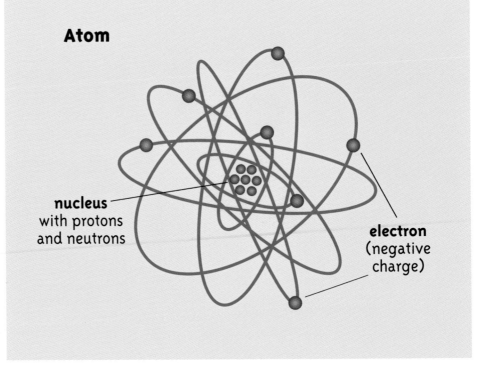

Atom

nucleus with protons and neutrons

electron (negative charge)

By the end of the 19th century scientists everywhere accepted that atoms were real, although an experiment by **J. J. Thomson** in 1899 showed that atoms contain electrons, proving atoms can be further divided. In 1911 the proton was recognized as a part of each atom, while in 1932 a third **subatomic particle**, the neutron, was found necessary in all but the simplest atoms. Starting in 1913, **Niels Bohr** developed the concept of the atom that most people have—a small central region of protons and neutrons clinging to each other (the nucleus) surrounded by electrons in orbit. Chemists have shown that this idea is too simple and the modern view has electrons in fuzzy clouds about the nucleus.

During this long history, no one had ever seen an atom. Since 1955, however, special microscopes have made individual atoms visible.

🖥📖 RESOURCES

- Stwertka, Albert. *The World of Atoms and Quarks.* New York: Twenty-First Century, 1995. (JUV/YA)
- "THE ATOM'S FAMILY": MONSTERS AND NIGHT CREATURES TELL OF THE ATOM.
  http://www.miamisci.org/af/sln/
- THE FIZZICS FIZZLE GUIDE TO PHYSICS.
  http://library.thinkquest.org/16600/beginner/atoms.shtml

Auenbrugger, Leopold

Physician: developed medical percussion
Born: November 19, 1722, Graz, Austria
Died: May 17, 1809, Vienna, Austria

 Early physicians depended mainly on the words of their patients when making a diagnosis. Their examinations of a patient's body were superficial

and they lacked techniques that could detect possible changes within the body.

One of the first such techniques was developed by Auenbrugger, who described it in a 1761 scientific paper. Called percussion, it involves tapping on a patient's chest and listening to the resulting sounds. Auenbrugger realized, for example, that the sounds of lungs full of air differ from those of lungs full of fluid. He used percussion to detect the presence of pneumonia, tuberculosis, and other respiratory disorders.

Auenbrugger's technique was neglected until around 1806, when Jean Nicolas Corvisart [French: 1775–1821] translated his paper and introduced percussion to physicians and medical students in Paris, among them **René Laënnec**, who would later invent the stethoscope.

Auroras

People who live nearer the poles than the equator often see colored lights in the night sky. The lights usually look like moving curtains of green light, but may also be red, blue, or yellow. They are the auroras ("dawns," although unconnected to sunrise), also called the northern lights (*aurora borealis*) or southern lights (*aurora australis*). The further north or south, the more frequently auroras appear.

Because auroras shine from polar regions, people first thought auroras might be ice-reflected sunlight, but in 1867 Anders Ångström [Norwegian: 1814–1874] showed that auroral light does not resemble sunlight. Measurements taken from the ground revealed that auroras start high in the **atmosphere**—in the electrically charged ionosphere. By 1931, scientists predicted that Earth's magnetic field interacts with the ionosphere to produce auroras, although the mechanism was unknown. Extensive auroras appeared in 1957–1958, just as early **artificial satellites** first encountered bands of high-speed charged particles collected by Earth's magnetic field. Particles from these bands—the Van Allen radiation belts—crash into the ionosphere near the magnetic poles, lighting up auroras.

RESOURCES

- Shepherd, Donna Walsh. *Auroras: Light Shows in the Night Sky*. New York: Franklin Watts, 1995. (JUV/YA)

- MORE ABOUT AURORAS.

  http://www.pfrr.alaska.edu/pfrr/aurora/INDEX.HTM

Automation

JACQUARD (weaving with punch cards) ➤ **Spencer** (Hartford automatic tools) ➤ industrial robots developed

In automation, tools manufacture products with little or no supervision by humans. As early as the 13th century, mills for grinding grain, preparing cloth, or obtaining metals from ores sometimes moved materials from one step to the next automatically.

Steps toward more complete automation began in the 19th century. In 1805, **Joseph-Marie Jacquard** introduced his method of controlling weaving with punched cards, later used to control early computers. In 1873, Christopher M. Spencer [American: 1833–1922] developed the first machine that not only moved

Auroras are created when the Earth's radiation belts interact with the ionosphere.

materials through it, but also changed tools automatically as the product was made. Tools of this type, called "Hartford automats" gradually became widespread. Around the same time, the chemical industry began to develop manufacturing plants that produced finished chemicals from raw materials with little or no human intervention—a system later adopted by oil refineries.

In 1954, automated factories for devices ranging from aluminum strips and iron engine blocks to entire radios were built, sometimes replacing a hundred human workers with one. Industrial **robots**, tools that can be pro-grammed for various tasks, were intro-duced in 1962.

Office automa-tion—the use of machines for producing, copying, or trans-mitting documents, developing charts, and so forth—differs from manufacturing automation, since humans decide how to proceed at each step. Computer-assisted design of devices is also considered a form of automation.

RESOURCES

Jefferis, David. *Artificial Intelligence: Robotics and Machine Evolution*. New York: Crabtree, 1999. (JUV/YA)

Thro, Ellen. *Robotics: The Marriage of Computers and Machines*. New York: Facts on File, 1993. (JUV/YA)

Automobiles

OTTO (introduced automobile engine) ➤ **DAIMLER** (developed automobile engine) ➤ **Benz** (first automobile) ➤ **Ford** (Model T/assembly line), **Dunlop** (rubber tires), **Olds** (mass production), **Kettering** (self-starter)

From the time that engines could convert chemical energy into motion, people have used engines to propel vehicles. When such a vehicle travels on roads or highways and carries passengers as its primary function, it is often called an automobile ("self-moving"). This is such a broad definition that it includes steam car-riages (the earliest in 1769 carried up to four people at walking speeds), electric vehicles, and several types of automobile that use internal combustion engines. The same technology is also used for vehicles, such as golf carts, tractors, motorcycles, and trucks, that we do not class as automobiles.

The overwhelming majority of auto-mobiles today use a form of engine similar to one introduced by **Nikolaus August Otto** in 1877 and developed further by **Gottlieb Daimler** in 1883. In 1885, Karl Benz [German: 1844–1929] installed a gasoline-powered version of this engine on a three-wheeled vehicle that is often considered the first true automobile. Daimler soon built a four-wheeled version, as did Benz. Commercial production of such vehicles started in France in 1890. By 1894, however, these gasoline-powered automobiles had to compete with electric cars and steam-powered road vehicles, often called steamers. Electric-powered automobiles were fastest, but could not travel long distances without recharging their batteries. Steamers were most powerful, but sometimes exploded, were dangerous in collisions, and had a high initial cost. Although some electrics and steamers operated as late as the 1920s, the gasoline-powered internal combustion engine dominated the automobile scene beginning with the Model T of 1908, designed by Henry Ford [American: 1863–1947].

The modern automobile has taken shape based on many separate inventions. Air-filled rubber tires were introduced in 1888 by John Boyd Dunlop [British: 1840–1921]; mass production by Raymond. E. Olds [American: 1864–1950] in 1901; both disk and drum brakes and the speedometer in

"Hot rods" of today are a combination of many automobile technologies, including fuel injection and high-tech braking systems.

Modern cars are streamlined to reduce air resistance.

1902; the self-starter by Charles Kettering [American: 1876–1958] in 1911; the automotive assembly line by Henry Ford in 1913; windshield wipers in 1916; streamlining in the Chrysler Airflow of 1934; the first form of automatic transmission in 1939; power steering in 1951; fuel-injection engines in 1966; and so forth.

Gasoline-powered internal combustion engines have remained dominant, but other means of power continue to be used. Gasoline-turbine engines of the 1950s were only demonstration models, but the automotive diesel engine, introduced by Rolls Royce in 1963, has gradually acquired more and more adherents because of its less expensive operating costs. In recent years, concerns about air pollution and petroleum supplies have renewed interest in electric automobiles, especially gasoline-electric hybrids. The hybrids have two engines, and part of the power from the gasoline engine keeps batteries charged to run the electric engine.

RESOURCES

- Corbett, David. *Automobiles* (The History Series). Hauppage, NY: Barrons Juveniles, 1999. (JUV/YA)
- Otfinoski, Steve. *Behind the Wheel: Cars Then and Now*. Tarrytown, NY: Benchmark, 1997. (JUV/YA)

Avery, Oswald Theodore

Physician, bacteriologist: showed genes consist of DNA
Born: October 21, 1877, Halifax, Canada
Died: February 20, 1955, Nashville, Tennessee

In the 1940s, Avery decided to expand on experiments performed by Frederick Griffith [English: 1879?–1941] in 1928. Griffith had studied two strains of the bacterium *Streptococcus pneumoniae*. One strain was virulent, causing pneumonia that quickly killed mice; the other strain was harmless. But when Griffith mixed dead virulent bacteria with living harmless bacteria and injected the mixture into mice, the mice died. Some substance in the dead bacteria had entered the living bacteria and changed them into killers. This "transformation factor" was passed on to future generations of bacteria, suggesting that it was part of the genetic material.

Avery and his colleagues broke down dead virulent bacteria and isolated the

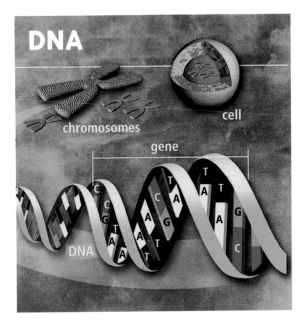

transformation substance. Then they chemically analyzed it. They found it was a nucleic acid—not protein, as was widely believed at the time. Avery named the substance deoxyribonucleic acid, or **DNA**. He and his associates presented their evidence in a famous paper published in 1944. The paper inspired numerous scientists, including **James Watson** and **Francis Crick**, to study DNA, and started a revolution in genetics that continues to this day.

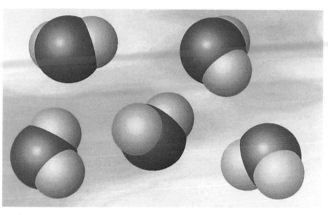

Molecules consist of two or more atoms bonded together.

 **RESOURCES**

- Lagerkvist, Ulf. *DNA Pioneers and Their Legacy.* New Haven, CT: Yale University, 1998.
- THE QUEST FOR DNA.

  http://esg-www.mit.edu:8001/esgbio/ dogma/history2.html
- THE BIRTH OF MOLECULAR BIOLOGY.

  http://esg-www.mit.edu:8001/esgbio/ dogma/old/dna.html

Avogadro, Amedeo

Physicist, chemist: formulated gas law
Born: August 9, 1776, Turin, Italy
Died: July 9, 1856, Turin, Italy

 At the beginning of the 1800s, there was no system for determining the formulas and atomic weights of gases. In 1811, Avogadro proposed an explanation that came to be called Avogadro's law. He said that two gases of the same volume at the same temperature and pressure contain the same number of particles. He called these particles "molecules," defining the term as the smallest unit of a substance that has all the properties of that substance. Since molecules of most gases consist of two or more atoms, molecular weight is the sum of the weights of all the atoms in a molecule. Using his law, Avogadro established that a molecule of water consists of two atoms of hydrogen and one atom of oxygen.

The actual number of molecules in a volume of gas is calculated using Avogadro's number, which usually is written as 6.022×10^{23}—shorthand for 602,200,000,000,000,000,000,000. This is the number of molecules of a gas contained in six gallons (22.7 liters).

Scientists ignored Avogadro's ideas until 1860, when Stanislao Cannizzaro [Italian: 1826–1910] reintroduced them at a famous conference in Germany. Scientists began to calculate correct atomic weights and **Dmitri Ivanovich Mendeleyev** was inspired to formulate the periodic table.

RESOURCES

- Nye, Mary Jo. *Before Big Science: The Pursuit of Modern Chemistry and Physics, 1800–1940.* Cambridge, MA: Harvard University, 1996.
- AMEDEO AVOGADRO (1776–1856): ESSAY ON A MANNER OF DETERMINING THE RELATIVE MASSES OF THE ELEMENTARY MOLECULES OF BODIES, AND THE PROPORTIONS IN WHICH THEY ENTER INTO THESE COMPOUNDS.

  http://maple.lemoyne.edu/giunta/ avogadro.html

Babbage, Charles

Mathematician: designed first computer
Born: December 26, 1792, London, England
Died: October 18, 1871, London, England

 Babbage was a mathematics student at Cambridge University when he first wished for a machine that could calculate mathematical tables. A decade later, in 1823, he designed just such a machine to perform calculations and print the tables on metal plates. Called the Difference Engine, it was to be powered by a steam engine and operated by a hand crank. Babbage built a model but abandoned the project when he realized the complete machine would weigh about two tons and require thousands of precisely made parts.

YEARBOOK: 1828

- Babbage becomes Lucasian Professor of Mathematics at Cambridge-the same professorship once held by **Isaac Newton**.
- **Friedrich Wöhler** is the first to make an organic compound from inorganic materials.
- **Karl Ernst von Baer** describes how the egg cells of vertebrates develop into embryos.

In the 1830s, Babbage began work on an even more ambitious machine, the Analytical Engine. Like a modern **computer**, it was designed to perform any kind of arithmetic operation. Instructions would be fed into the machine on cards with holes punched in them, and there would be a memory unit in which numbers could be stored. Many consider this machine the first computer. The most enthusiastic supporter of the project was **Ada Lovelace**, who, said Babbage, "seems to understand it better than I do." But because of financial and other problems, Babbage never built the Analytical Engine.

RESOURCES

- Collier, Bruce and James MacLachlan. *Charles Babbage and the Engines of Perfection.* New York: Oxford University, 1999. (JUV/YA)
- CHARLES BABBAGE INSTITUTE.
  http://www.cbi.umn.edu

Bacon, Roger

Philosopher and monk: the first modern scientist
Born: c. 1214, Ilchester, England
Died: June 11, 1292, Oxford, England

Bacon is considered by many to have been the first modern scientist. He believed that the way to learn about nature is to observe carefully, carry out experiments, and keep accurate records—not just accept what other people say. Bacon's superiors in the Church did not agree with this philosophy. They demanded that he write only about things that met their approval; after Bacon disobeyed, he was imprisoned.

FAMOUS FIRST

Bacon was the first person known to use gunpowder in Europe. After hearing about "black powder" from people who had traveled to China, Bacon mixed charcoal, sulfur, and potassium nitrate together. In 1242, he wrote, "If you light it you will get thunder and lightning if you know the trick."

Roger Bacon

Bacteria

 VAN LEEUWENHOEK (first observation) ➤ **Ehrenberg** (name) ➤ **Cohn** (classification) ➤ **KOCH/PASTEUR** (bacterial disease) ➤ **EHRLICH** (syphilis drug) ➤ **FLEMING** (first antibiotic) ➤ **Winogradsky** (bacterial metabolism), **Beijerinck** (nitrogen cycling)

Bacteria are among the oldest forms of life. However, people did not know of their existence until the

Timeline of Bacteria

1676	Leeuwenhoek discovers bacteria
1838	Ehrenberg recognizes bacteria as a distinct group of organisms
1857	Pasteur shows that some bacteria carry out fermentation
1857	Pasteur proposes "germ theory" of disease
1875	Cohn publishes early classification of bacteria
1876	Koch demonstrates that anthrax is caused by a particular bacterium
1881	Pasteur develops an anthrax vaccine
1883	Koch shows that tuberculosis is caused by a specific bacterium
1885	Pasteur develops vaccine against rabies
1888	Beijerinck isolates *Rhizobium* bacteria that live in nodules on roots of peas and other legumes
1889	Winogradsky determines that some bacteria use hydrogen sulfide as an energy source
1890	Winogradsky isolates nitrifying bacteria in soil
1899	Beijerinck discovers that something smaller than a bacterium also can cause disease; he calls it a **virus**
1910	Ehrlich introduces chemical treatment that kills syphilis bacteria
1928	Fleming discovers an antibiotic that kills bacteria

Bacon devoted much time to studying optics and the human eye. He described eyeglasses, imagined the possibility of microscopes, telescopes, and flying machines, which weren't built until much later. By spraying water into the air he showed that rainbows are created when sunlight hits drops of moisture. Bacon was also interested in chemistry—he showed that air is needed for combustion and demonstrated how to purify potassium nitrate (saltpeter).

17th century, following the invention of the **microscope**. Bacteria were first observed by **Antoni van Leeuwenhoek** in 1676. In 1683, he made drawings of various kinds of bacteria he saw in scrapings taken from his teeth.

The name "bacterium" (sing.) was introduced by Christian G. Ehrenberg [German: 1795–1876] for one particular group of bacteria (pl.); later, this name came to be used for the more general class of microorganisms. The first scientist to publish a comprehensive classification of different kinds of bacteria, dividing them into genera and species, was Ferdinand Cohn [German: 1828–1898].

While scientists such as Cohn were studying the structure of bacteria, other scientists were studying the effects of these organisms. Around 1880, **Robert Koch** and **Louis Pasteur** proved that some

FAMOUS FIRST

Not all bacteria are harmful. The advent of **genetic engineering** made it possible to use bacteria to produce certain human substances. This was first done in 1979, when the gene for human insulin was inserted into the common bacterium *Escherichia coli. E. coli* divides about once every 20 minutes. Soon there were millions of bacteria carrying the gene and making human insulin. This process—today carried out in huge vats—ensures a plentiful supply of insulin for diabetics, who cannot make enough of their own.

bacteria cause **disease**. This instigated the search for ways to combat such bacteria. Pasteur developed a **vaccine** for rabies, **Paul Ehrlich** found a "magic bullet" that killed syphilis bacteria, and **Alexander Fleming** discovered the first **antibiotic**.

Bacterial waste in water

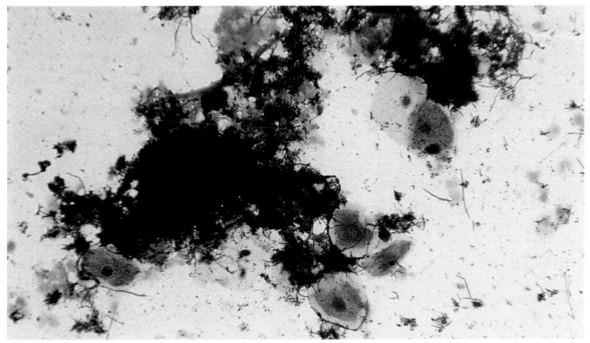

The study of bacterial **metabolism** was pioneered by Sergius Winogradsky [Russian: 1856–1953], who found species that could survive without oxygen. This led to many valuable discoveries, such as that by Martinus Beijerinck [Dutch: 1851–1931] showing that bacteria play a critical role in cycling nitrogen through the environment.

See also classification of life.

 **RESOURCES**

• BACTERIA: LIFE HISTORY AND ECOLOGY.

  http://www.ucmp.berkeley.edu/bacteria/bacterialh.html

• MICROBIOLOGY.

  http://www-micro.msb.le.ac.uk/109/History.html

• THE MICROBIAL WORLD.

  http://helios.bto.ed.ac.uk/bto/microbes/shape.htm#crest

Baekeland, Leo Hendrik

Chemist: invented first completely synthetic plastic
Born: November 14, 1863, Ghent, Belgium
Died: February 23, 1944, New York, New York

 Baekeland left his native Belgium to seek his fortune in the United States in 1889 and just ten years later found it. Eastman Kodak bought the rights to an improved photographic paper he had invented for $1,000,000—a fortune at that time.

Baekeland's second major invention brought him lasting fame. While searching for an insulator to replace natural shellac, he found a way to combine a coal-tar derivative, phenol, with formaldehyde to make a hard, strong, moldable material that he called

Bakelite. Once Bakelite had been solidified through heating, it was stable and non-reactive. After Bakelite was introduced in 1909, it replaced wood, metal, and celluloid (a flammable plastic made from wood) in thousands of applications. Bakelite and its imitations were the beginning of the modern plastics industry.

 **RESOURCES**

• TIME MAGAZINE'S 100 GREAT PERSONS OF THE 20TH CENTURY.

  http://www.time.com/time/time100/scientist/profile/baekeland.html

A radio made from Bakelite

Baer, Karl Ernst von

Zoologist: pioneered modern study of embryos
Born: February 17, 1792, Piep, Estonia
Died: November 28, 1876, Dorpat, Russia

By the early 1800s, people had seen the eggs of many animals, but never those of mammals.

Many scientists believed that a completely formed mammal existed in miniature within the material that developed into an embryo and then a newborn. This erroneous idea was discarded after 1826, when Baer discovered egg cells in female mammals.

Baer went on to prove that all animals,

Baer drew this illustration in 1827 to compare a mammalian egg to that of other animals, such as lizards, frogs, and crabs.

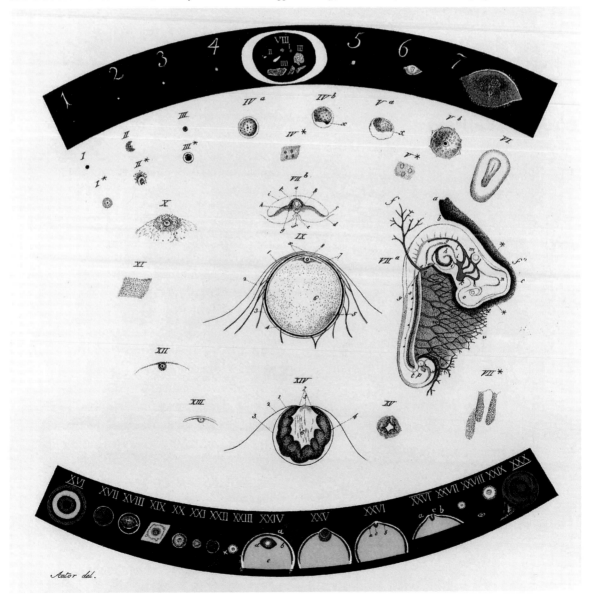

including humans, develop from a single egg cell. He observed how an egg cell divides to form a multicellular embryo with different layers of tissue, each giving rise to specific organs. He also compared embryos of different kinds of animals, showing that they resemble one another in the early stages of development.

RESOURCES

- Oppenheimer, Jane M., ed. *Autobiography of Dr. Karl Ernst von Baer*. Canton, MA: Watson, 1986.
- BIOGRAPHY OF KARL ERNST VON BAER.
  http://www.zbi.ee/baer/biography.htm

Baeyer, Adolf von

Chemist: discovered barbiturates and synthesized the dye indigo
Born: October 31, 1835, Berlin, Germany
Died: August 20, 1917, Starnberg, Germany

Adolf von Baeyer

 Early in his long career, Baeyer studied uric acid, from which he derived an acid that he is said to have named for his girlfriend Barbara. Barbituric acid, discovered in 1863, led to a class of drugs called barbiturates, widely used as drugs to calm nerves or induce sleep.

During the later years of the 19th century, Baeyer turned his attention to the main problems of organic chemistry at that time—dye production and the structure of carbon-based compounds. He was successful in both efforts. He synthesized the plant-derived blue dye indigo in 1880 and then determined its structure. He also developed general rules that explained why carbon tends to form rings of five or six atoms rather than some other number.

In 1871, Baeyer found a gummy resin produced by combining phenol and formaldehyde, but ignored it as he was seeking dyes, not resins. Almost 40 years later, **Leo Hendrik Baekeland** turned the same resin into the first synthetic plastic.

NOBEL PRIZE 1905

Baeyer won the Nobel Prize in chemistry in 1905 "in recognition of his services in the advancement of organic chemistry and the chemical industry."

RESOURCES

- MORE ABOUT BAEYER.
  http://www.scs.uiuc.edu/mainzv/Web_Genealogy/Info/baeyerajfwr.pdf
  http://www.nobel.se/chemistry/laureates/1905/baeyer-bio.html

Baird, John Logie

Inventor: first to broadcast television
Born: August 13, 1888, Helensburgh, Scotland
Died: June 14, 1946, Bexhill, England

 In 1925, Baird was the first to transmit recognizable images of humans. He improved a device invented in 1884 by Paul Nipkow [German: 1860–1940], in which a rapidly spinning disk lets light through a pattern of holes while a photoelectric cell responds to changes in light intensity with a variable electric current. A second Nipkow disk reproduces the original image by converting current back into light.

FAMOUS FIRST

The first person to make money transmitting pictures over wires was Giovanni Caselli [Italian: 1815–1891]. His electro-mechanical devices carried pictures from Paris to two other French cities, starting in 1865 but ending in 1870 when France was disrupted by war.

Like Nipkow, Baird transmitted images over wires, first at a London department store, then between London and Glasgow, and even from London to New York, using telephone lines. He then combined his methods with radio to produce what we recognize today as television. In 1929, he persuaded the British Broadcasting Corporation to start experimental television broadcasts. Although all-electric systems of television developed by other inventors soon replaced the rotating disks, Baird was the first person to make regular television broadcasts.

RESOURCES

- Reid, Struan. *John Logie Baird*. Westport, CT: Heinemann, 2000. (JUV/YA)
- MORE ABOUT JOHN LOGIE BAIRD.

  http://arts.uwaterloo.ca/FINE/juhde/hills961.htm

  http://www.digitalcentury.com/encyclo/update/baird.html

Ballard, Robert

Marine scientist: found the *Titanic*
Born: June 30, 1942, Wichita, Kansas

Ballard is famous for his discovery in 1985 of R.M.S. *Titanic*, the ocean liner that hit an iceberg and sank beneath the cold, dark waters of the North Atlantic in 1912. But his interest in exploring the oceans began many years earlier, when as a child he read Jules Verne's *20,000 Leagues Under the Sea*—it "really kindled a fire inside of me, making me think, I can do that. I can be an explorer too!" Ballard has said.

In the early 1970s, Ballard participated in the first manned exploration of the mammoth underwater mountain range known as the Mid-Atlantic Ridge. In 1979, he and his team discovered "black smokers" —deep-ocean hot springs surrounded by dense concentrations of gigantic tube-worms and other exotic creatures.

Ballard helped develop deep-sea sleds that are pulled along the ocean floor by a ship on the surface. The sleds can carry cameras to transmit video pictures to the towing ship. Ballard used them to locate several major shipwrecks, including the *Titanic*; the U.S.S. *Yorktown*, which sank in World War II; and the first two intact ancient Phoenician ships ever found. The

Jason, a remotely operated vehicle, is equipped with TV cameras and a sample-retrieving mechanism.

remotely operated vehicle *Jason*, named for the mythical Argonaut sailor, is a centerpiece of the JASON Project, which Ballard founded in 1989 to connect youngsters worldwide to his yearly explorations.

See also diving technology.

 **RESOURCES**

• Ballard, Robert D., with Rick Archbold. *The Discovery of the Titanic; Exploring the Greatest of All Lost Ships*. New York: Warner, 1998

• Ballard, Robert D., with Will Hively. *The Eternal Darkness: A Personal History of Deep-Sea Exploration*. Princeton, NJ: Princeton University, 2000.

• Ballard, Robert D, with Rick Archbold. *Ghost Liners: Exploring the World's Greatest Lost Ships*. Boston: Little, Brown, 1998. (JUV/YA)

• INTERVIEW WITH ROBERT BALLARD.

http://americanhistory.si.edu/csr/comphist/ballard.html

Balloons

THE MONTGOLFIER BROTHERS (first balloon) ➤ CHARLES (hydroden balloon) ➤ Giffard (propeller-driven balloon) ➤ von Zeppelin (dirigible)

People from early times noticed that smoke rises and takes light objects, such as dried leaves, with it. In France, the **Montgolfier brothers** used this power of fire to lift heavier objects. They made bags and filled them with hot air. When they were filled, the bags lifted into the sky—the first balloons. In 1783, the Montgolfiers built a large balloon that flew two passengers over Paris for nearly a half-hour.

That same year, French chemist **Jacques Alexandre Charles** developed a balloon that used a light hydrogen gas for lifting power. After he learned of the Mongolfiers' steam engine turning a propeller to direct the balloon. This was the first use of a propeller in air (instead of in water, on ships).

Dirigibles are airships that can be steered. The dirigible *La France*, powered by an electric engine, was launched in 1884. It was the first dirigible that could be flown back to its takeoff point. Dirigibles manufactured by Ferdinand von Zeppelin [German: 1838–1917], starting in 1900, were lifted by hydrogen, had rigid frames

hot-air balloon, Charles also flew passengers late in 1783.

Balloon riding became an overnight craze. One balloon carried a rider over the English Channel in 1785. In 1794, a French army officer used a balloon to spy on the enemy during a battle, which contributed to a French victory. Military balloons, with various purposes, have continued to be used since.

A propeller-driven balloon is called an airship. **Steam engines** were too heavy for the earliest balloons, but in 1852, Henri Giffard [French: 1825–1882] built a balloon 144 feet (44 m) long that employed a small

Hot-air balloons are popular for recreation today.

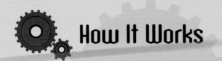

How It Works

Balloons are based on a principle first stated by Archimedes: an object in a fluid is lifted by a force equal to the difference between the weight of the object and the weight of the same volume of fluid. A boat floats in water for the same reason. A volume of heated air, hydrogen, or helium weighs less than the same volume of unheated air. When the balloon and its load weigh a little less than the air displaced, the whole rig—balloon, gondola, and passengers—floats in air. Air at higher altitudes becomes lighter per volume, so managing either the total weight of the entire rig or the volume inside the balloon allows it to float at different heights.

inside the balloons, internal combustion engines, and large passenger gondolas fitted out like luxury liners. "Zeppelins" were used successfully, even providing regular transatlantic service until 1937 when the fire and crash of the *Hindenberg* in New Jersey demonstrated the danger of highly flammable hydrogen.

In 1915, the British military developed a simpler form of dirigible, the B-limp, or blimp. The "limp" part of the name means that there is no rigid frame. Blimps still have some military uses but today most carry advertising messages.

 RESOURCES

• HISTORIES OF BALLOONING.

http://www.skywalker.at/faq.htm

http://www.bris.ac.uk/Depts/Union/BUHABS/history.htm

http://www.exploratorium.edu/ls/balloons/balloonhistory.html

Banting, Frederick

Physician, medical researcher: isolated insulin
Born: November 14, 1891, Alliston, Ontario, Canada
Died: February 21, 1941, Newfoundland, Canada

Even before he received his medical degree, Banting was interested in diabetes mellitus. Several researchers had suggested that this disease is caused by a lack of insulin, a **hormone** produced by certain cells in the pancreas. Attempts had been made to supply diabetic patients with insulin by feeding them ground-up pancreases. These experiments failed, apparently because during the preparation process trypsin—an enzyme normally secreted through ducts in the pancreas—destroyed the insulin.

Banting had an idea: Might it be possible to extract insulin if the ducts of the pancreas

Frederick Banting

NOBEL PRIZE 1923

Banting and Macleod were awarded the Nobel Prize in medicine or physiology "for their discovery of insulin." Banting divided his share of the money with Best. Macleod split his portion with Collip.

were tied? In 1921, working in the laboratory of John J.R. Macleod [Scottish: 1876–1935] at the University of Toronto, Banting began to test his ideas. He was helped by a graduate student, Charles Best [Canadian: 1899–1978]. Banting and Best soon obtained an insulin extract, but only in small, impure amounts. Chemist James B. Collip [Canadian: 1892–1965] came to their assistance, devising a method of purifying the insulin. When patients were injected with the purified insulin extract their health quickly improved. The treatment of diabetes was changed forever.

Notable Quotable

It occurred to me when we were puffing up the hill and the train was speeding along away below that the engine with all its power could not go up that slushy, soft, snowy road as fast as we could. Power is useless unless directed in the proper channel. People have different powers and the big question in life must be—"Are we on the right road for travel?" We will certainly not get far in our given time unless we have chosen the road that is fitted to our particular locomotive.

—Frederick Banting

🖥️📖 RESOURCES

• Bliss, Michael. *Banting, a Biography*. Tonawanda, NY: University of Toronto, 1992.

• BIOGRAPHY OF BANTING.

  http://www.nobel.se/medicine/laureates/1923/banting-bio.html

• DSCOVERY OF INSULIN.

  http://www.discoveryofinsulin.com/

Bardeen, John

Physicist: co-invented the transistor
Born: May 23, 1908, Madison, Wisconsin
Died: January 30, 1991, Boston, Massachusetts

In 1947, Bardeen was working at Bell Telephone Laboratories in New Jersey with two other physicists, William Shockley [American: 1910–1989] and Walter Brattain [American: 1902–1987]. They were studying the properties of semiconductors—certain crystalline solids, such as silicon, through which electrons can flow—in hopes of finding a solid-state equivalent of vacuum tubes. Their research led them to invent the **transistor**, a semiconductor device that can amplify electric current. The transistor radically changed **computers**, making them smaller and much more practical.

Bardeen moved to the University of Illinois in 1951. There, in 1958, he and two of his students, Leon Cooper [American: 1930–] and J. Robert Schreiffer [American:

NOBEL PRIZE 1956

Bardeen, Shockley, and Brattain shared the Nobel Prize in physics for inventing the transistor.

From left: William Shockley, John Bardeen, and Walter Brattain accept a gold medal from INTERCON's Seymour Schweber.

1931–], presented the first theory to explain successfully the **superconductivity** of materials at extremely low temperatures. It is known as the BCS theory, after their initials.

~~~>>>>>}}}){{{{<<<<~~~

NOBEL PRIZE 1972

Bardeen, Cooper, and Schreiffer shared the Nobel Prize in physics for their work on superconductivity.

RESOURCES

- Riordan, Michael and Lillian Hoddeson. *Crystal Fire: The Birth of the Information Age.* New York: W.W. Norton, 1997.
- BIOGRAPHY OF JOHN BARDEEN.
  http://www.nobel.se/physics/laureates/1972/bardeen-bio.html
- JOHN BARDEEN, WILLIAM SHOCKLEY, WALTER BRATTAIN.
  http://invent.org/book/book-text/5.html

Bates, Henry Walter

Naturalist: discovered animal mimicry
Born February 8, 1825, Leicester, England
Died February 16, 1892, London, England

Thanks to excellent skills of observation, Bates discovered that unrelated species of animals living in the same area may have similar colors and patterns—a phenomenon now called Batesian mimicry. In 1848, Bates left his job in his father's stocking factory and sailed to Brazil with his friend **Alfred Russel Wallace**. The two men shared a deep interest in nature and they planned to study and collect tropical plants and animals. Wallace returned to England in 1852, but Bates remained until 1859.

During his 11 years in Brazil, Bates explored the entire Amazon River valley and collected more than 14,000 species, mostly insects previously unknown to science. Among these insects were pairs of butterfly species with similar coloration. One species of each pair is dangerous or has an awful taste. The second species—the mimic—is harmless and tasty, but predators mistake it for the other species and leave it alone.

 **RESOURCES**

• BATES IN THE AMAZON, 1863.

  http://abacus.gene.ucl.ac.uk/jim/Mim/Bates63.html

Batteries

💡 **GALVANI** (early observation) ➤ **VOLTA** (first electric battery) ➤ **Daniell** (wet cell) ➤ **Planté** (automobile battery) ➤ **Leclanché** (dry cell)

 How It Works

Some electrons in metals float loose from atoms. In pairs of metals suitable for batteries, one loses electrons that the other accepts. A salt solution is neutral but contains equal numbers of mobile positive and negative charges. Charges in the solution transport electrons from one metal to the other. Placing a conductor between the two metals allows current to flow.

The story of the battery begins in 1786, when **Luigi Galvani** observed a frog's muscle twitch as it touched two different metals. **Alessandro Volta** recognized that the electricity powering the twitch came from the metals. In 1800, Volta obtained the first continuous electric current, using zinc and silver linked by salt water. It was the first electric battery—a device to convert chemical energy into electric current.

Many types of batteries have been invented since 1800. A version developed

Batteries come im many shapes and sizes.

in 1836 by John Daniell [English: 1790-1845], known as the wet cell or Daniell cell, uses copper in copper sulfate and zinc in zinc sulfate. It was the main laboratory source of power for decades. The common automobile battery, created by Gaston Planté [French: 1834–1889] in 1859, can be recharged by reversing a chemical reaction between lead and sulfuric acid. The flashlight battery, based on an 1868 invention of Georges Leclanché [French: 1839–1882], is called a dry cell because it contains slightly damp paste instead of liquid. Different batteries are designed for long life, high power, or recharging ease, depending on the application.

RESOURCES

- Borton, Paula and Vicky Cave. *The Usborne Book of Batteries and Magnets.* Tulsa, OK: EDC, 1995. (JUV/YA)
- Marshall Brain's "How Stuff Works."

  http://www.howstuffworks.com/battery.htm

Beagle Expedition

Began: December 27, 1831
Ended: October 2, 1836

"The voyage of the *Beagle* has been by far the most important event in my life," wrote **Charles Darwin** in his autobiography. The *Beagle* was a British navy ship that sailed from England in late 1831 on an expedition that would circumnavigate the world. During the next five years, its crew surveyed and made maps of the coasts of southern South America, visited islands in the Pacific Ocean, and set up a chain of stations for measuring time. But the expedition's most significant contribution was its influence on Darwin.

The ship's captain, meteorologist Robert FitzRoy [English: 1805–1865], wished to have a naturalist along. Darwin volunteered his services. He was young and lacked experience, but he was enthusiastic and willing to travel without salary. The expedition gave him many opportunities to observe living organisms in their natural environments—as well as fossils, coral reefs, volcanic islands, and other phenomena. He collected numerous specimens; for example, on a single day in Brazil, he collected 68 different kinds of beetles.

When the *Beagle* visited the Galapagos Islands, Darwin noticed that giant tortoises on different islands had different shapes and colors. He saw a variety of finches that looked almost identical but had different beaks suited to different lifestyles. These observations gradually led him to develop his theory of **evolution**.

Giant Galapagos tortoises were among the many animals that Darwin observed on the **Beagle** *expedition.*

 **RESOURCES**

• Darwin, Charles. *The Voyage of the Beagle.*
  Amherst, MA: Prometheus, 1999. Also available
  at **http://www.literature.org/authors/
  darwin-charles/the-voyage-of-the-
  beagle/preface.html**

Beaumont, William

Surgeon and physiologist: first to observe human
  digestion
Born: November 21, 1785, Lebanon, Connecticut
Died: April 25, 1853, St. Louis, Missouri

"I have availed myself of the opportunity afforded by a concurrence of circumstances which probably can never again occur," noted Beaumont. The unusual circumstances began in 1822 when Beaumont treated a young Canadian, Alexis St. Martin, who had been accidentally shot in the abdomen. Beaumont pushed his organs back into place and covered the opening in the body wall. St. Martin soon got well, but his wound failed to close completely, leaving a permanent hole in his stomach.

Beginning in 1825, St. Martin sporadically allowed Beaumont to use him to study the process of digestion. For example, at intervals after St. Martin dined, Beaumont would insert a tube through the hole and take samples of the stomach contents. In another experiment, Beaumont tied small pieces of various foods to the ends of strings, inserted them through the hole, then withdrew what was left at hourly intervals to observe the rate of digestion.

In 1833, Beaumont published his experiments and observations. He described the movements of the stomach, showed that gastric juice is produced when food comes in contact with the stomach wall, and noted that weather conditions can affect stomach temperature. Beaumont's work revolutionized understanding of digestion and influenced many other researchers in the field of **physiology**.

RESOURCES

• Beaumont, William and William Osler.
  *Experiments and Observations on the Gastric
  Juice and Physiology of Digestion,with a
  Biographical Essay, "William Beaumont: A
  Pioneer American Physiologist."* Mineola, NY:
  Dover, 1996.
• Horsman, Reginald. *Frontier Doctor: William
  Beaumont, America's First Great Medical
  Scientist.* Columbia: University of Missouri, 1996.
• LIFE OF WILLIAM BEAUMONT.

  http://www.james.com/beaumont/dr_life.htm

Becquerel, Antoine Henri

Physicist: discovered radioactivity
Born: December 15, 1852, Paris, France
Died: August 25, 1908, La Croisic, France

Becquerel's father had studied fluorescence—light emitted by materials as a result of exposure to **ultraviolet radiation**. In November 1895, **Wilhelm Konrad Röntgen** discovered X rays. Becquerel immediately hypothesized that fluorescent materials, which produce light on exposure to X rays, might release the new form of radiation themselves. Becquerel chose fluorescent crystals of uranium salts and obtained what appeared to be positive results. After exposure to sunlight, the uranium produced invisible radiation that could penetrate opaque paper to make images on photographic film.

Cloudy weather several days in a row halted the experiments. Becquerel stored the uranium with the film in a dark closet

Antoine Henri Becquerel

Behring, Emil von

Bacteriologist: co-discovered antitoxins
Born: March 15, 1854, Hansdorf, Germany
Died: March 31, 1917, Marburg, Germany

Behring began his career as a physician in 1880, a year that saw his homeland devastated by an epidemic of diphtheria. It was a time when scientists were just discovering that certain infectious diseases are caused by **bacteria**. Behring was eager to develop ways to combat the microorganisms. He investigated an iodine compound, iodoform, and found that, though it did not kill bacteria, it appeared to neutralize poisons produced by the bacteria.

In 1884, Friedrich Löffler [German: 1852–1915] isolated the bacterium that

Emil von Behring

while waiting for sunlight. After several dark days, he tired of waiting. On March 1, 1896, he developed the film. Although the uranium crystals had not been exposed to sunlight, the image was strong, because uranium emits radiation without an input of energy. Other physicists rushed to study the new rays, which in 1898 **Marie Curie** named "**radioactivity**." Becquerel himself found in 1899 that, unlike X rays, radiation from uranium bends in a magnetic field. He concluded that this meant that the radiation consisted of electrons. This was true, although it was only part of the story.

RESOURCES

• MORE ABOUT ANTOINE HENRI BECQUEREL.

http://www.orcbs.msu.edu/radiation/
radhistory/antoinebecquerel.html

http://www.nobel.se/physics/
laureates/1903/becquerel-bio.html

causes diphtheria. Then **Pierre Paul Émile Roux** and Alexandre Yersin [French: 1863–1943] showed that this bacterium does its damage by excreting a poison, which they called a toxin.

Behring recalled the effects of iodoform and wondered if something could be found to neutralize diphtheria toxin. Working in the laboratory of **Robert Koch**, he and **Shibasaburo Kitasato** discovered that small doses of sterilized diphtheria bacteria cause an animal's blood to produce a substance that protects against the toxin. They called the substance an antitoxin, and demonstrated that diphtheria antitoxin produced by one guinea pig can be used to provide other guinea pigs with **immunity** against the disease.

NOBEL PRIZE 1901

Behring received the first Nobel Prize in physiology or medicine for developing a "victorious weapon against illness and deaths."

 **RESOURCES**
- BIOGRAPHY OF EMIL ADOLF VON BEHRING.
http://www.nobel.se/medicine/ laureates/1901/behring-bio.html

Bell, Alexander Graham

Inventor: developed telephone and other useful devices
Born: March 3, 1847, Edinburgh, Scotland
Died: August 2, 1922, Beinn Bhreagh, Nova Scotia

 Bell's family specialized in speech therapy. From age 15 on, Bell learned about mechanisms of speech and sound from his father and grandfather.

Bell had read in 1863 that **Hermann von Helmholtz** transmitted tones using electrical currents, magnets, and a tuning fork. Bell experimented in reproducing more complex sounds, using rapidly varying currents through wires to turn electromagnets on and off. The magnets vibrated metal reeds that were tuned to match the current's frequencies, producing sounds. Bell's

Alexander Graham Bell

harmonic telegraph of 1875, based on this system, transmitted several messages at the same time over a single wire.

In 1876, Bell replaced the metal reeds with a metal membrane and found that he could reproduce speech. The first transmission of a voice message was to his assistant Thomas A. Watson [American: 1854-1934] in a nearby room. Bell's request, "Mr. Watson, come here—I want to see you," became the first words spoken over the new device, the telephone. A few months later, Bell spoke to his father over a tele-phone line 8 miles (13 km) long. By the end of 1876, he had extended the length of this telephone line to 143 miles (230 km).

Bell withheld patenting his telephone at the request of a British investor. His father-in-law, however, applied for the patent in Bell's name—only two hours before the application of another inventor, Elisha Gray [American: 1835–1901], whose device was nearly identical. A ten-year battle followed, with Bell finally winning what has been called the most financially important patent in U.S. history.

Bell continued to be an inventor all his life. In 1880, he invented the photophone, which was a device for transmitting sounds with light. He also built metal detectors for locating bullet fragments in the human body, one of which was used when U.S. President James Garfield was shot in 1881. In 1886, Bell greatly improved Thomas Alva Edison's phonograph by using waxed cylinders and wavy grooves to record sounds.

Bell later became interested in flight and developed new forms of kites. He started a group of aviation inventors who developed the hydrofoil, still used on speedboats and some transport ships.

Bell also helped found the magazine *Science* in 1880 and was president of the National Geographic Society from 1898 to 1904.

YEARBOOK: 1876

- Telephone is patented.
- **Bicycle** with a chain to the back wheel is introduced.
- First practical refrigerator is invented.
- Electric arc light that can burn for two hours is developed.

RESOURCES

- Matthews, Tom and Gilbert Grosvenor. *Always Inventing,*. Washington, DC: National Geographic, 1999.
- MacLeod, Elizabeth. *Alexander Graham Bell: An Inventive Life*. Toronto: Kids Can, 1999.
- BELL'S NOTEBOOKS AND BIOGRAPHY.
  http://jefferson.village.virginia.edu/albell/homepage.html

Bell Burnell, Jocelyn

Astronomer: discovered pulsars
Born: July 15, 1943, Belfast, Ireland

 Bell Burnell was a research student working under the supervision of Antony Hewish [English: 1924–] in 1967 when she began surveying the universe using a **radiotelescope** she helped to build. One night she detected a rapid series of pulsating radio waves occurring at regular intervals. She jokingly called them LGMs—Little Green Men—and suggested they might be some form of radio wave interference, or perhaps signals from life on a distant planet.

During the following months, Bell Burnell showed that the signals were

Jocelyn Bell Burnell

Notable Quotable

Finding the first one was quite a bit of worry because it was so unexpected—it had to be man-made, there had to be something wrong with the equipment, it had to be interference, it had to be satellites in the orbit. With so many things that we had to check out it was really quite a headache, [fearing] that we were spending all these hours checking out something and it would turn out to be utterly mundane and we would have literally wasted that time. But finding the second one, that justified the point.

—Jocelyn Bell Burnell

coming from a source outside the solar system. She located three additional sources of pulsating radio waves, and it became apparent that she had discovered a previously unknown phenomenon. Hewish named the sources "pulsating **stars**"—a name since shortened to pulsars. Thomas Gold [Austrian-American: 1920–] proposed that they are small, rapidly spinning neutron stars, a theory confirmed in 1968. Hundreds of pulsars are now known.

NOBEL PRIZE 1974

The first Nobel Prize in physics ever awarded for astronomical research was shared by Hewish, for the discovery of pulsars, and Martin Ryle [English: 1918–1984], for observations and inventions in radio astronomy.

RESOURCES

- INTERVIEW WITH JOCELYN BELL BURNELL.
  http://www.nmt.edu/kweather/bell.html

Benedict, Ruth

Anthropologist: compared human cultures
Born: June 5, 1887, New York, New York
Died: September 17, 1948, New York, New York

"Each great culture has taken a certain direction not taken by another," proposed Benedict. Based on research among Native American peoples, she suggested that cultures are organized around religious and other beliefs, and that these are important in determining the personalities of members in a culture. For example, she showed that some cultures promote peaceful cooperation while others promote aggression.

A graduate of Vassar College, Benedict was in her early thirties when she fell in love with **anthropology**—the study of human cultures. In 1921, she entered Columbia University to study under Franz

Ruth Benedict

YEARBOOK: 1934

- Benedict's *Patterns of Culture*, which sets forth her concept of cultures, is published.
- **Irène and Frédéric Joliot-Curie** develop the first artificial radioactive element.
- **Wernher von Braun** launches a **rocket** 1.5 miles into the sky.

Boas [German-American: 1858–1942], the first major anthropologist in the United States and also the teacher of **Margaret Mead**. After receiving her doctorate degree, Benedict remained at Columbia for the rest of her life, first as a lecturer, then as a professor.

During World War II, the U.S. government asked Benedict to use her skills to study Japanese culture. She described her findings in *The Chrysanthemum and the Sword* (1946), a bestseller that influenced U.S. policy toward Japan during the postwar years.

RESOURCES

- Benedict, Ruth, et al. *Patterns of Culture*. Reissue ed. Boston: Houghton Mifflin, 1989.
- Ruth Fulton Benedict.
  http://www.webster.edu/woolflm/ruthbenedict.html

Berliner, Emile

Inventor: developed disk phonograph record
Born: May 20, 1851, Hannover, Germany
Died: August 3, 1929, Washington, D.C.

Soon after **Alexander Graham Bell** invented the telephone in 1876, Berliner developed a more effective version of Bell's device for changing sound into electric current. The process and Berliner's flat disk were combined in 1904 to create a basic form of recording sound and playing it back. This process was later replaced by the inventions of magnetic tape in 1932 and compact disk in 1982.

 RESOURCES

• INVENTOR'S HALL OF FAME.

   http://www.invent.org/book/book-text/
   9.html

Bernoulli, Daniel

Physicist and mathematician: discovered how a
   fluid's velocity changes its pressure
Born: February 8, 1700, Groningen, Netherlands
Died: March 17, 1782, Basel, Switzerland

Bernoulli came from a large family of Swiss mathematicians who worked in various European nations in the 17th and 18th centuries. His father Jean and uncle Jacques together created whole new branches of mathematics.

Daniel, who contributed to oceanography and astronomy as well as mathematics, is best known for his work in physics. In 1738, he established Bernoulli's principle that a fluid produces less pressure as its velocity increases, an effect that provides much of the lift for airplanes. He was also the first to use the idea that a gas is made from tiny, invisible particles as a way to derive the properties of gases, properties that were discovered experimentally by **Robert Boyle**, **Blaise Pascal**, and other early scientists.

RESOURCES

• MORE ABOUT DANIEL BERNOULLI.

   http://www-groups.dcs.st-and.ac.uk/
   history/Mathematicians/Bernoulli_Daniel.html

Emile Berliner

Bell Telephone Company bought his invention and hired Berliner.

Bell, Berliner, **Thomas Alva Edison**, and other inventors competed to improve the new inventions of the day. Edison independently invented the same telephone transmitter as Berliner, for example. The original versions of telephones, phonographs, electric lights, and motion pictures had many flaws. Edison's first phonographs recorded sound as hills and valleys on a cylinder covered with foil. Bell improved the sound and stability of cylinder recording by replacing the up-and-down impressions with a back-and-forth groove preserved in shellac, a natural resin often called "wax." In 1887, Berliner also used back-and-forth grooves, but he devised a way of chemically etching the groove onto a disk. Bell's wax

Bicycles

Two-wheeled hobbyhorse ➤ **France** (célerifère) ➤
Niepce (célerifère redesign) ➤ **Scotland** (addition
of treadles and levers) ➤ **France** (crank handle/pedal)
➤ Velocipede ➤ Air-filled rubber tires

The bicycle began as a toy for the rich, evolved into a form of transportation, became a toy for children, and today is all of these things as well as the basis of a popular sport.

Near the end of the 18th century, children sometimes played on a two-wheeled hobbyhorse propelled by pushing their feet on the ground. In 1790, a French count built an adult version that he called the célerifère ("quick strike"), which was briefly popular with the nobility. After the French Revolution and reign of Napoleon I, Joseph Nicéphore Niepce [French: 1765–1833], better known as the creator of the first photographs, redesigned the célerifère, which then (1816) became generally popular in Paris. Enthusiasm increased when an 1818 version was manufactured that could be steered by turning the front wheel.

Between pushes, a person balanced a célerifère without his or her feet touching the ground. In 1839, a Scottish blacksmith designed a version using treadles and levers, similar to the levers turning the wheels of a steam locomotive, that carried power to the back wheel as the rider balanced. French inventors had a better idea, which was to develop a speed advantage by using the foot to turn a crank handle that was attached to the front wheel. With each foot pushing a crank half way around, the pedal was born in 1861. Pedals turning in a relatively small circle rotated the much larger wheel, and the vehicles were called velocipedes ("swift-footed"). Since the ratio

Today, bicycles come in a wide variety of shapes, sizes, and designs.

of pedal radius to front wheel radius determined speed, versions with very large front wheels were developed. But the giant front wheels made the velocipede unstable and accidents were common.

Also, only riders with long legs could reach the pedals.

In 1869, manufacturers began to use chains to allow a rider placed between the wheels to pedal the velocipede. In 1885, the safety bicycle, manufactured by the Rover Company in England, became the standard, with two equal-sized wheels and pedal power transmitted by a covered chain to the back wheel. Air-filled rubber tires were invented in 1888 and gears became available as early as 1890.

Bicycles prepared the way for **automobiles**, especially by necessitating better **roads**. People trained as bicycle mechanics became the inventors of the automobile, and bicycle manufacturers switched to making cars.

In the latter part of the 20th century, the sport of bicycle racing led to many improvements in bicycles. The environmental movement promoted the use of bicycles as clean, energy-efficient transportation. Specialized bicycles were developed for riding on trails and up mountains.

RESOURCES

- LW Books. *Evolution of the Bicycle, vol. 1 & 2.* Marion, IN: LW Books, 1998.
- Otfinoski, Steve. *Pedaling Along: Bikes Then and Now.* Tarrytown, NY: Benchmark, 1997. (JUV/YA)
- Oxlade, Chris. *Bicycles.* Westport, CT: Heinemann, 2000. (JUV/YA)
- BICYCLE RULES FROM SAN FRANCISCO.
  http://www.tmasf.org/bicycles.htm
- THE ILLINOIS LEAGUE OF BICYCLISTS.
  http://www.bikelib.org/Bicycles/Bicycles.html

Binney, Edwin

Inventor: developed Crayola crayons
Born: 1866
Died: 1934

 Binney revolutionized people's use of color. His enthusiasm for red iron oxides led to the American custom of painting barns red. His work with carbon black led to its use in printing inks, paints, and automobile tires. Best of all, Binney created modern crayons.

Binney and his cousin C. Harold Smith [English-American: 1860–1931] headed Binney & Smith, a company that specialized in pigments and related chemical compounds. They entered the school market around 1900, selling slate pencils. Soon thereafter they developed the first dustless chalk for classroom blackboards. When Binney

Edwin Binney

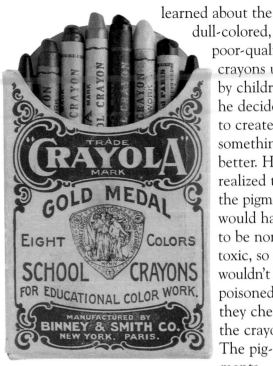

learned about the dull-colored, poor-quality crayons used by children, he decided to create something better. He realized that the pigments would have to be non-toxic, so kids wouldn't be poisoned if they chewed the crayons. The pigments would have

First box of Crayola crayons, 1903.

to mix easily with wax, to ensure a uniform color. The wax would have to be strong enough to form slim cylinders that could be held in young hands. By 1903, Binney and his researchers had created Crayola crayons.

RESOURCES

- Woods, Samuel G. *Crayons from Start to Finish*. Woodbridge, CT: Blackbirch Press, 1999.
- INVENTORS OF THE WEEK: EDWARD BINNEY & HAROLD SMITH.
  http://web.mit.edu/invent/www/crayons.html
- THE COLORS OF CHILDHOOD.
  http://www.smithsonianmag.si.edu/smithsonian/issues99/nov99/object_nov99.html

Bioluminescence

Homer (early observation), **Aristotle** (early observation), **Pliny the Elder** (early observation)
➤ **Dubois** (chemical nature) ➤ Applications

People have known for thousands of years that some organisms produce light, or bioluminescence. Homer [Greek: c. 12th century B.C.E.] called sparkles he saw in the ocean "phosphorescence of the sea." **Aristotle** wondered why mushrooms glowed in the dark. Pliny the Elder [Roman: c. 23–79] described how certain clams "shine in one's mouth as one chews them."

The first person to recognize the chemical nature of bioluminescence was French physiologist Raphael Dubois. In the 1880s

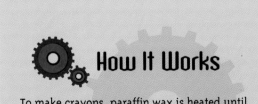

How It Works

To make crayons, paraffin wax is heated until it liquefies, then mixed with powdered pigment. The mixture is poured into cylindrical molds. Water is used to cool and solidify the wax. When crayons are solid they are ejected from the molds and sent to a machine that wraps and glues on labels.

FAMOUS FIRST

One of the best-known bioluminescent organisms is the firefly, which uses flashes of light to signal potential mates. In 1990, Wayne Barnes [American: 1947–] introduced the firefly's luciferase gene into tobacco plant cells. The cells grew into tobacco plants that glowed a neon green after being given luciferin. Such bioluminescent "tags" have become very useful in genetic research.

Light signals are an important means of communication in the animal world.

he conducted experiments with bacteria and isolated two substances. One he named luciferin. The second, an enzyme that catalyzes the reaction of luciferin with oxygen to product light, he called luciferase. Since then, dozens of different luciferins and luciferases have been discovered in bacteria, fungi, invertebrates and fish.

Other researchers investigated how organisms use bioluminescence. They discovered that light signals are an important means of communication, used to attract prey, warn predators, or signal potential mates.

Beginning in the late 1970s, scientists developed interesting applications for bioluminescence. For instance, **genetic engineering** can be used to create bioluminescent bacteria that work as detectives. Such bacteria light up when certain harmful chemicals are present in soil, water, or other materials.

RESOURCES

- Berger, Melvin. *Creatures That Glow: A Book about Bioluminescent Animals.* New York: Scholastic, 1996. (JUV/YA)

- Strasshofer, Craig. *Lights in the Night: Everything You Always Wanted to Know about Things That Glow.* Cleveland: Creativity for Kids, 1995. (JUV/YA)

Birdseye, Clarence

Inventor: invented quick freezing
Born: December 9, 1886, New York, New York
Died: October 7, 1956, New York, New York

 In 1912, after dropping out of college for financial reasons, Birdseye became a fur trader and went to Labrador, Canada. He saw that people there preserved food by freezing it. He noticed that food froze almost instantly in bitterly cold winter weather—and, when thawed, retained its flavor, texture, and

YEARBOOK: 1930

- Birdseye's company begins retail sales of frozen foods.
- **Philo Farnsworth** receives patents for his television system and receiver.
- Richard Drew [American: 1886–1956] receives patent for masking tape.

RESOURCES

- CLARENCE BIRDSEYE AND BIRDS EYE FROZEN FOODS.
  http://otal.umd.edu/vg/amst205.F97/vj30/project5.html
- INVENTOR OF THE WEEK: CLARENCE BIRDSEYE.
  http://web.mit.edu/invent/www/inventorsA-H/birdseye.html

color better than did food frozen more slowly during the milder spring and autumn. He realized that quick freezing didn't allow ice crystals to form and cause food cells to burst.

When Birdseye returned to the United States, he began experimenting with quick freezing. He developed a process for packing fresh food into waxed cardboard cartons, then rapidly freezing the contents under high pressure. His method, still basically in use, revolutionized the food industry.

An inveterate inventor, Birdseye held nearly 300 patents, including ones for infrared heat lamps, a food-dehydrating process, and a recoilless harpoon gun.

See also food preservation.

Black, Joseph

Chemist and physicist: discovered properties of carbon dioxide, concepts of latent and specific heat
Born: April 16, 1728, Bordeaux, France
Died: December 6, 1799, Edinburgh, Scotland

The study of both chemistry and physics leaped forward in the second part of the 18th century, due mostly to an ability to take careful measurements. Black was the first scientist to measure gases using precise weights and to employ accurate thermometers—invented by Daniel Fahrenheit [Polish-Dutch: 1686–1736] in 1714.

Joseph Black

Notable Quotable

I do not consider myself a remarkable person. I am just a guy with a very large bump of curiosity and a gambling instinct.

—Clarence Birdseye

Black studied changes caused by heating carbonate compounds, leading to his 1754 discovery of carbon dioxide. He observed that carbon dioxide is also produced by breathing, fermentation, and combustion.

In 1760, Black began investigating temperature changes in freezing and boiling. Over the next two years, his experiments showed that freezing water releases heat and melting removes heat from surrounding materials; similarly, boiling requires heat beyond the amount needed to raise temperature to the boiling point. The additional heat needed or released in boiling, freezing, melting, or condensing from vapor to liquid is called latent heat. Black also discovered that different materials respond differently to heating or cooling (specific heat).

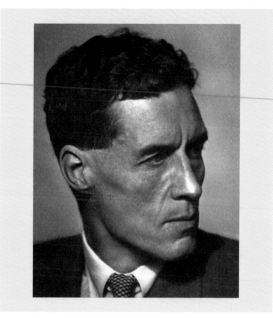

Patrick Blackett

Blackett, Patrick M.S.

Physicist: observed particle interactions and invented operations research
Born: November 18, 1897, London, England
Died: July 13, 1974, London. England

 After serving in the British navy during World War I, Blackett studied at Cambridge University. There he specialized in using a device called the cloud chamber to detect and record radiation. In 1924, he became the first to photograph one element—nitrogen—changing into another—oxygen. This process, called transmutation, was produced by exposure to a radioactive source. In 1932, Blackett

YEARBOOK: 1924

• Blackett observes transmutation of an element.
• The portable radio, Kleenex, and the self-winding watch are introduced.

studied cosmic rays passing through the cloud chamber. He became the first to observe matter—electrons and their antiparticles—arising out of pure energy unleashed by cosmic rays.

NOBEL PRIZE 1948

Blackett received the Nobel Prize in physics for developing improved methods for observing particle interactions.

During World War II, Blackett created the management method called operations research. Operations research uses mathematics to determine the best action among several choices. Blackett's analysis of bombing tactics greatly improved the ability of British planes to sink submarines. His method also made development of radar and nuclear weapons more efficient.

Boats

💡 Dugout canoe ➤ **Australia** (rafts or canoes) ➤ Animal skins stretched over frames ➤ **Egypt** (sails) ➤ **Egypt** ➤ Wooden boats with oars ➤ **Malaysia** (outrigger) ➤ Motorized boats

A boat is a floating means of transportation, usually unroofed and small, intended for use on streams, lakes, or near shore. Large water transports designed for travel over oceans are ships.

Most wood floats in water. A large piece of wood or several roped together form a raft that can carry humans and cargo. A bundle of reeds also makes a good raft. Rafts are, however, hard to steer or propel.

Removing part of the inside of a log creates the dugout canoe, the first boat. People settled Australia by traveling over deep water as early as 60,000 B.C.E., perhaps on rafts, but probably in canoes. Dugouts and their paddles from 7500 B.C.E. have been preserved in Northern European bogs. Canoes were also made from bark. Other early boats were animal skins stretched over frames.

In Egypt, by 3000 B.C.E., bundles of reeds were shaped into boats, paddled or propelled with simple sails. By 2500 B.C.E., Egyptians built boats of lumber that were probably rowed with oars (paddles that use the boat as a fulcrum). Most boats since have been improved designs of canoes and rowboats. The outrigger, a float attached to a canoe by a long rod, was invented in Malaysia sometime before 1000 B.C.E. The first high-speed internal combustion engine, built in 1883, was designed to propel a rowboat. This was the birth of motorized boats.

RESOURCES

- Greenhill, Basil and John S. Morrison. *The Archeology of Boats and Ships: An Introduction.* Annapolis, MD: United States Naval Institute, 1996.
- Kently, Eric. *Eyewitness: Boat.* New York: Alfred A. Knopf (DK Publishing), 2000. (JUV/YA)
- MESSING ABOUT IN BOATS.
  http://mims.com/maib/
- OUTRIGGER CANOES.
  http://www.ozemail.com.au/kanu/faq.html - anchor428247

Boats have been a part of human civilization for more than 60,000 years.

Bohr, Niels

Physicist: described atomic structure and interpreted quantum theory
Born: October 7, 1885, Copenhagen, Denmark
Died: November 18, 1952, Copenhagen, Denmark

 After studying surface tension in water, Bohr traveled to England in 1911 to work on electrons and atoms. He assisted **Ernest Rutherford** in showing that electrons orbit a central atomic nucleus and, in 1913, after returning to Denmark, used **quantum theory** to analyze atomic structure. His discovery that electrons occupy certain orbits only accounts precisely for lines in **spectroscope** images. In 1920, the Danish government created the Institute of Theoretical Physics in Copenhagen, which under Bohr became the leading center for quantum theory. Bohr's atomic theory predicted that an undiscovered element would be found mixed with zirconium. A 1923 search in zircon located the element, which was named hafnium after an ancient name for Copenhagen.

Niels Bohr

NOBEL PRIZE 1922

Niels Bohr received the Nobel Prize in physics for his analysis of electron orbits in hydrogen.

Nuclear fission was discovered in 1938 and the next year Bohr, drawing on his experience with surface tension, explained fission as similar to a large drop of water splitting in two. Bohr's theory showed that uranium-235 could power **nuclear weapons**, a result he brought to the United States, where he helped develop the atomic bomb.

In addition to producing specific mathematical theories, Bohr led the physics community in searching for the philosophical meaning behind quantum theory.

Notable Quotables

Our task is not to penetrate into the essence of things, the meaning of which we don't know anyway, but rather to develop concepts which allow us to talk in a productive way about phenomena in nature.

—Niels Bohr

An expert is a man who has made all the mistakes which can be made in a very narrow field.

—Niels Bohr

RESOURCES

• Spangenburg, Ray and Diane K. Moser. *Niels Bohr: Gentle Genius of Denmark.* New York: Facts on File, 1995.

• MORE ABOUT NIELS BOHR.

http://www-groups.dcs.st-and.ac.uk/history/Mathematicians/Bohr_Niels.html

Boomerangs and Bolas

The angled-wood boomerang, with a curving flight path that returns it to the thrower, is one of many devices that early humans developed to kill or capture small game by throwing something at it. Wooden tools often decay with no trace, so the first boomerang on record is an ivory one, carved from a mammoth tusk more than 25,000 years ago and found in Poland. A wooden boomerang preserved in a Polish cave dates from 19,000 years ago. The earliest known Australian boomerangs date from about 10,000 B.C.E. Not all boomerangs are designed to return to the thrower; those that are not are also called "throwing sticks."

The bola consists of two or three weights tied together with cord. The bola is whirled about for greater speed and then hurled. When the cord strikes, the weights whip around, wrapping the animal's legs and bringing it down. Although people associate bolas with 19th-century Argentine herders, bolas were used by Native Americans along the Columbia River in Washington about 6,000 B.C.E. and in South America as early as 5,000 B.C.E.

A stone tool called a hand ax was commonly used by very early ancestors of humans; many believe it was a throwing weapon, not an ax. Another early throwing weapon is the sling, a cord used as an extension of the arm to give a thrown stone greater power. Similarly, a wooden extension of the arm called a spear thrower or atlatl, invented by at least 15,000 B.C.E., makes it possible to hurl a short spear or harpoon with great force.

Borlaug, Norman

Agricultural scientist: launched the Green Revolution in farming
Born: March 25, 1914, near Cresco, Iowa

In 1944, Borlaug accepted an invitation to work on a project to improve wheat production in Mexico. At that time, Mexico had to import about half of the wheat it needed, a costly expense. For nearly 20 years, Borlaug and his team experimented with ways to control insects, improve soil, and breed plant varieties better adapted to a wide range of environmental conditions. They gathered and cross-bred wheats from around the world to create dwarf wheats that were disease-resistant and produced two to three times more grain than traditional varieties. Wheat production in Mexico soared and the nation soon was **farming** all the wheat it needed.

Borlaug then began training and working with agricultural scientists elsewhere. Food productivity improved dramatically

NOBEL PRIZE 1970

Borlaug won the Nobel Peace Prize for his success in boosting crop production and starting the Green Revolution.

during the 1960s—from India and the Philippines to the Middle East and sub-Saharan Africa—and Borlaug became known as the father of this "Green Revolution."

 RESOURCES

- BIOGRAPHY OF NORMAN ERNEST BORLAUG.

  http://www.nobel.se/peace/laureates/1970/borlaug-bio.html

- FOOD SECURITY: THE LIFE AND WORK OF NORMAN BORLAUG, NOBEL LAUREATE.

  http://www.rockfound.org/agsci/robertherdt.html

Bovet, Daniel

Pharmacologist: produced sulfonamide, antihistamines, and synthetic curare
Born: March 23, 1907, Neuchâtel, Switzerland
Died: April 8, 1992, Rome, Italy

Bovet's first important research involved the red textile dye Prontosil, which **Gerhard Domagk** had discovered fights *Streptococcus* bacteria in living organisms but not in test tubes. Bovet reasoned that an organism's cells must break down Protonsil, releasing a therapeutic compound. His experiments showed that this indeed happens. One of the Prontosil fragments is the bacteria-killer sulfonamide. It was possible to produce sulfonamide in quantity, and it became the first of the sulfa drugs that saved millions of lives during World War II.

Bovet next focused on histamine, a hormone that produces allergic reactions to irritants such as pollen. He made the first antihistamines (drugs that counteract histamine).

After World War II, Bovet studied curare, a plant substance used in arrow

poisons by South American peoples. Previously, researchers had shown that small doses of curare relax a patient's muscles

Daniel Bovet

prior to surgery. But curare was expensive—and unpredictable. Bovet produced more than 400 synthetic versions of curare, including succinylcholine, which can be used safely in surgery.

 **RESOURCES**

- BIOGRAPHY OF DANIEL BOVET.

  http://www.nobel.se/medicine/laureates/1957/bovet-bio.html

Bow and Arrow

Spain (stone arrowheads) ➤ **Africa** (rock art images of archers) ➤ **Europe** (arrow shafts) ➤ **Italy** (catapult) ➤ **China** (crossbow)

The bow for shooting arrows was invented after the spear and boomerang. The earliest known stone arrowheads, found in Spain, date from about 16,000 B.C.E. Rock art in north Africa showing archers was drawn about that same time. The earliest arrow shafts are preserved in bogs in northern Europe, some from as early as 8000 B.C.E., and in an Alpine glacier from about 3300 B.C.E.

Bows have more uses than launching arrows. Wrapping the cord around a shaft and pushing the bow back and forth rotates the shaft at high speeds. This idea was used, probably starting about 8000 B.C.E., for drilling holes and starting fires with friction.

About 400 B.C.E. two adaptations of the bow were introduced. In Italy, Greek inventors developed a large bow pulled by teams of soldiers that could launch heavy stones or spears—the catapult. Catapults sent missiles over walls or even through them. In China, a smaller, handheld device employed a similar idea. The crossbow shoots a heavy arrow, called a bolt. The user cocks the bow (perhaps using a pulley for added power) and can unleash at will. By the 1st century C.E., the crossbow was known in Greece and Rome. In the middle ages, improved crossbows were so deadly that the Church tried to outlaw them. After guns were introduced, however, bows and crossbows gradually ceased being used as weapons of war. Today they are mainly used in target shooting or for hunting deer and other large game.

RESOURCES

• Hardy, Robert. *Longbow: A Social and Military History*. New York: Arco, 1976 (reprint by Bois D'Arc, 1998).

• HISTORIES OF LONGBOW AND CROSSBOW.

  http://www.gci-net.com/users/w/wolfsoul/medieval/longbow/longbow.html

Most modern bows and arrows are made from lightweight metals, instead of wood.

Boyle, Robert

Physicist and chemist: introduced laws of gases
and basic concepts of chemistry
Born: January 25, 1627, Lismore Castle, Ireland
Died: December 31, 1691, London, England

 Boyle was among the founders of Britain's Royal Society, chartered in 1663, one of the most influential scientific organizations. He also practiced and promoted what has become the scientific method, based on experiment, careful records, cooperation with other scientists, and full publication of data. The influence of these practices was as important as his many discoveries.

Robert Boyle

Assisted by **Robert Hooke**, Boyle built an improved air pump, which allowed him to discover, in the early 1660s, many properties of both air and the vacuum. He developed Boyle's law, which states that the pressure of a gas varies with its volume. He observed that sound cannot be transmitted nor charcoal burn in a vacuum. He studied **bioluminescence** and found that it does not occur in a vacuum either. He also introduced improved versions of such scientific tools as the hydrometer, for measuring density of liquids, and the camera obscura, for projecting an image onto paper.

His 1663 book *The Sceptical Chymist* proposed that elements are made from atoms that can be combined to form compounds, which are different from mixtures. He introduced chemical methods for distinguishing between **acids and bases**. He also, in 1680, invented the first match based on friction and chemicals.

RESOURCES

Sargent, Rose-Mary. *The Diffident Naturalist: Robert Boyle and the Philosophy of Experiment.* Chicago: University of Chicago, 1995.

• Tiner, John Hudson. *Robert Boyle: Trailblazer of Science.* Fenton, MI: Mott Media, 1989.

• MORE ABOUT ROBERT BOYLE.

  http://www.bbk.ac.uk/boyle/index.html
  http://www.oxy.edu/terhakop/boyle.html

Brain

Hippocrates (brain as seat of intelligence) ➤
Flourens (functions of cerebellum), **Hitzig/Fritsch**
(cerebral cortex regions associated with specific
responses) ➤ Amino acids influence brain function

 People in ancient times knew of the brain, though they did not agree on its function. The earliest known

Major Parts of the Human Brain

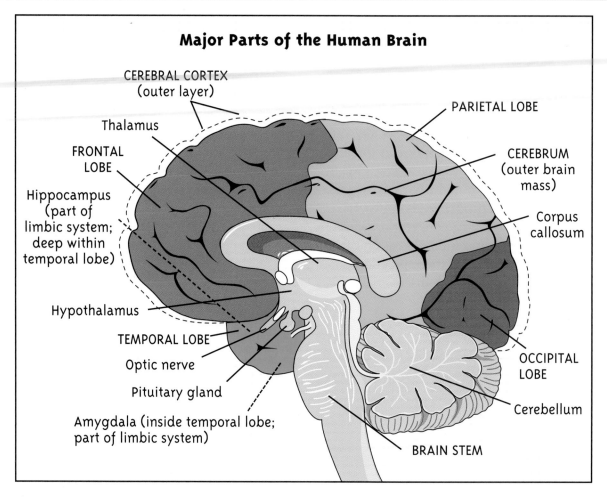

CEREBRAL CORTEX (outer layer)

Thalamus

FRONTAL LOBE

Hippocampus (part of limbic system; deep within temporal lobe)

Hypothalamus

TEMPORAL LOBE

Optic nerve

Pituitary gland

Amygdala (inside temporal lobe; part of limbic system)

PARIETAL LOBE

CEREBRUM (outer brain mass)

Corpus callosum

OCCIPITAL LOBE

Cerebellum

BRAIN STEM

document using the word "brain" was a papyrus written in Egypt around the year 1700 B.C.E. The papyrus described the brain's general **anatomy** and the meninges (tissues) that cover it.

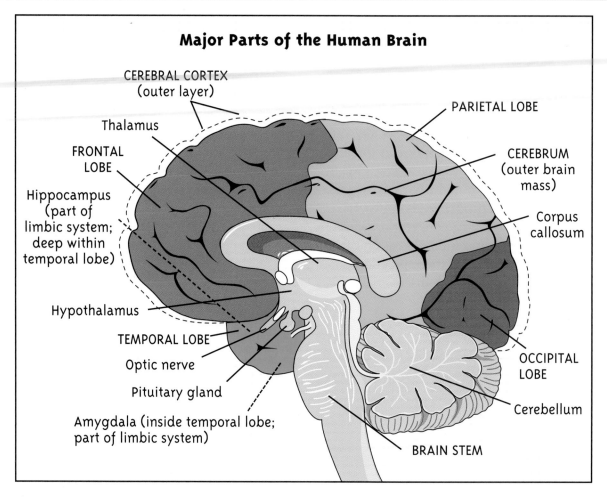

NOBEL PRIZE 2000

Arvid Carlsson [Swedish: 1923–], Eric R. Kandel [Austrian-American: 1929–], and Paul Greengard [American: 1925–] shared the Nobel Prize in physiology or medicine for discoveries concerning transmission of signals between brain cells.

In ancient Greece, **Hippocrates** said the brain was the seat of intelligence and involved with the senses. However, **Aristotle** believed the heart was the center of intelligence and thought. Other erroneous ideas, such as that nerves are hollow tubes carrying fluid, were perpetuated for centuries.

It wasn't until the 19th century that people began to learn about the brain's functions and understand that this organ, with the help of the nervous system, supervises and coordinates all body activities. Microscopic studies showed that the brain consists of many different kinds of cells. Development of galvanometers enabled scientists to prove that nerve cells give off an electrical charge when transmitting messages. Jean Pierre Flourens [French: 1794–1867] discovered the functions of the cerebellum. Eduard Hitzig [German: 1838–1904] and Gustav Fritsch [German: 1838–1927] demonstrated that specific regions of the cerebral cortex are associated with specific responses.

Technological advances during the 20th century sped developments in neurology (study of the brain and nervous system). The left and right hemispheres of the cerebrum were found to have different functions. Researchers determined the chemical composition of brain cells, showed that certain amino acids influence brain function, and demonstrated the role of chemicals in the transmission of nerve impulses. They began to understand the effects of various drugs on brain activity.

RESOURCES

- Greenfield, Susan. *The Human Brain*. New York: Basic, 1998.
- BRAIN FACTS AND FIGURES.
  http://faculty.washington.edu/chudler/ facts.html
- FOUNDERS OF NEUROLOGY.
  http://www.uic.edu/depts/mcne/founders/

Braun, Wernher von

Rocket engineer: designed V-2 and Saturn rockets
Born: March 23, 1912, Wirsitz, Germany
Died: June 16, 1977, Alexandria, Virginia

 As a youngster, Braun dreamed of building rockets and exploring space. An early influence was *The Rocket into Interplanetary Space*, a 1923 book by Hermann Oberth [Romanian-German: 1894–1990] that suggested the use of liquid-propellant rockets for spaceships. Another important influence was **Robert Hutchings Goddard.**

By 1934, Braun was launching rockets more than 1.5 miles (2.4 km) into the sky. With Adolf Hitler's rise to power, all non-military rocket research ended and Braun became the technical director of Germany's program to develop military rockets. He was the main designer of the V-2, a liquid-fuel rocket that could carry a warhead to a target 500 miles (800 km) away. It was the first successful long-range ballistic missile and also the first human-made object to reach altitudes above 50 miles (80 km), the height at which outer space begins.

After World War II, Braun moved to the United States. He worked on the U.S. army's ballistic-weapon program and helped build the Redstone rocket, which launched the first U.S. **artificial satellite**, *Explorer 1*, into orbit on January 31, 1958. Next, Braun headed the team that developed the Saturn rockets, including *Saturn V*—the rocket that put *Apollo* astronauts on the Moon beginning in 1969.

RESOURCES

- Bilstein, Roger E. *Stages to Saturn: A Technological History of the Apollo/Saturn Launch Vehicle*. Upland, PA: Diane, 1999.
- Miller, Ron. *History of Rockets*. Danbury, CT: Franklin Watts, 1999. (JUV/YA)
- Otfinoski, Steven. *Blasting Off: Rockets Then and Now*. Tarrytown, NY: Marshall Cavendish, 1998. (JUV/YA)
- MORE ABOUT WERNHER VON BRAUN.
  http://www.archives.state.al.us/famous/ academy/w_braun.html

Bridges

💡 Fallen logs ➤ Arched bridges ➤ Stone bridges ➤ **Greece** (floating bridge) ➤ **Gaul** (wooden trestle bridge) ➤ **Pennsylvania** (first modern suspension bridge)

 Fallen logs across streams were surely the first bridges. Firmly anchoring the bridge, or span, at each end helps keep it in place during high water. Wider streams can be bridged with short spans between supports in the stream, although if natural islands are not present, such supports are hard to build in running water. Better bridges rise far above a stream, allowing boats to pass beneath them.

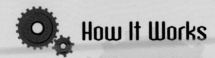

How It Works

Although the roadway of a short bridge can be supported at each end only, a longer bridge needs more support. Weight-bearing arches leave openings underneath while supporting the bridge above. Frames can support bridges from above or below. Trestle bridges often have light, openwork frames below them as supports. In a suspension bridge, the roadway is suspended from cables attached to towers above.

Bridges formed by arches are known from as early as 850 B.C.E., and later

Below left: San Francisco's Golden Gate Bridge is one of the world's most famous suspension bridges. **Below right, top:** *Arched stone bridge.* **Below right, bottom:** *Wooden pier bridge.*

Timeline of Bridges

B.C.E.

850 First arch bridge

600 Drawbridge over the Euphrates River in Asia

19 3 tiers of arches appear in the Pont du Gard bridge in Nîmes, France

C.E.

610 Segmented arch bridge over the Chiao Shui River in China (still stands)

1176 Construction of first London Bridge over Thames River started; completed in 1209

1560 Elliptical arch bridge is introduced, crossing the Arno River in Italy

1607 Pont Neuf bridge, the oldest still in use in Paris, is completed

1685 The caisson, a barrier to water while a pier is built in a river, is introduced

1779 A cast-iron bridge over the Severn River in England is first iron bridge

1792 A modern wooden truss bridge is built over the Merrimack River in Massachusetts

1809 A suspension bridge spanning 244 feet (74 m) is built across the Merrimack

1825 Thomas Telford builds a suspension bridge with a span of 579 feet (176 m)

1855 Roebling completes 841-foot (250-m) suspension bridge over the Niagara River

1883 Brooklyn Bridge over East River in New York completed; main span is 1,595 feet (486 m) long

1889 Forth railway bridge in Scotland is first large bridge built of steel

1904 Reinforced concrete is used for a bridge in Germany

1929 Twisted prestressed cables are introduced on the Grand'Mère Bridge in Quebec, Canada

1931 George Washington Bridge over the Hudson River in New York spans 3,500 feet (1,067 m)

1937 Golden Gate Bridge in San Francisco spans 4,200 feet (1,280 m)

1977 Longest steel-arched bridge, spanning 3,030 feet (924 m) crosses New River in West Virginia

1981 Bridge over Humber River in England spans 4,626 feet (1,410 m)

1986 Cable-stayed bridge in Canada spans 1,525 feet (465 m), first very large bridge to be suspended from cables attached directly to high towers.

1998 Great Belt suspension bridge in Denmark spans 5,328 feet (1,624 m)

Tatara Bridge in Japan is cable-stayed bridge with 2,920-foot (890-m) span.

Akashi Kaikyo in Japan becomes suspension bridge with longest span, 6,532 feet (1,991 m)

became widely used in the Roman empire. The earliest stone bridge of consequence, crossed the Euphrates River on seven pillars about 600 B.C.E., spanning 380 feet (116 m). One section was a drawbridge that could be lifted for boats to pass or to prevent hostile forces from crossing. In the wars between the Greeks and Persians a hundred years later, the Persian army used a floating bridge to invade Greece. By 50 B.C.E., Julius Caesar's army crossed the Rhone to invade northern Gaul on a wooden trestle bridge that they built themselves.

Today, most long bridges are suspension bridges. Pre-Columbian suspension bridges in the Andes remained in use until the 19th century. The first modern suspension bridges were a 1796 footbridge in Pennsylvania and an 1809 bridge across the Merrimack River in Massachusetts. The heyday of the suspension bridge began with an 1855 bridge constructed by John Augustus Roebling [German-American: 1806–1869] over the

Niagara River at Niagara Falls and his
Brooklyn Bridge of 1869–1883, completed by
his son Washington Roebling [American:
1837–1926]. The longest bridge today is a
suspension bridge in Japan, spanning 6,532
feet (1,991 m).

 **RESOURCES**

• Delony, Eric. *Landmark American Bridges*.
Boston: Bullfinch, 1993.
• Ostrow, Steven A. *Bridges*. London: Metro, 1997.
• MORE ABOUT BRIDGES.
http://www.struct.kth.se/research/bridges/
Bridges.htm
http://www.discovery.com/stories/
technology/buildings/bridges.html

Bronze and Brass

Copper refined from ore ➤ **Mesopotamia** (copper
utensils) ➤ Other metals added to copper to make
bronze ➤ Tin and copper ➤ Copper and aluminum
➤ Brass

The alloy bronze was the first metal
to have an important role in human
history, although first people used
copper refined from ore (smelted). Copper
was used for knives and other utensils from
about 2500 B.C.E. to 3000 B.C.E. in
Mesopotamia and
even later in both
Egypt and Europe.
About 3000 B.C.E., met-
alworkers discovered that
adding other metals or ores to
copper ore lowered the
heat required for smelting
and produced a harder,
stronger product—bronze.
Originally, tin and copper
ores were combined
to make the best

*Many statues, like this one of George Washington, are made
of bronze, which develops a greenish patina with time.*

bronze, but tin ore is much less common
than copper ore. Soon tin was smelted
where it was mined, notably in Cornwall
(southwestern Great Britain), and shipped
elsewhere to be added to metallic copper.

Other metals also hardened copper. Tin-
poor Egyptian smelters made bronze with
copper and arsenic ore. Today corrosion-
resistant bronze is made with copper and
aluminum.

Soon after the end of the Bronze Age—
about 1000 B.C.E. in Greece and the
Middle East—another alloy of copper was

discovered. A small amount of copper smelted with zinc ore produces a large amount of a bright gold metal that is easily worked into many shapes—brass. Brass became the first choice for coins as well as for many ornamental purposes. It remains popular for the latter.

See also mining.

Brown, Robert

Botanist: discovered Brownian movement and the cell nucleus
Born: December 21, 1773, Montrose, Scotland
Died: June 10, 1858, London, England

In 1827, Brown was observing pollen grains under a microscope. The grains were suspended in water and Brown saw that they moved about in a constant, random manner. He experimented with other substances, including scrapings from his teeth and coal dust. He suggested

How It Works

In 1905, **Albert Einstein** showed that Brownian movement occurs because the particles are constantly being hit by naked-to-the-eye water molecules. Each time a particle is hit, it moves.

correctly that the phenomenon, today known as Brownian movement, occurs whenever very fine particles are suspended in a fluid.

Brown's second major discovery came the following year. In the course of looking at orchid tissue under his microscope, he saw a dark, circular spot in each **cell**. He named it the nucleus and noted that while there is no regularity as to its place in the cell, it often is centrally located.

Buckyballs

Kroto (carbon in space is different from diamond or graphite) ➤ **Smalley** (created carbon molecules) ➤ 12 pentagonal faces ➤ Fullerenes and nanotubes ➤ Soot contains fullerenes

Since 1772 it has been known that the element carbon appears in several distinct forms, including transparent diamond, easily split black graphite, and powdery soot, thought to be crumbled graphite. The difference between diamond and graphite is simply how the carbon atoms link together. In 1985 two different studies came together to reveal that carbon atoms link together in another way, forming spheres known as "buckyballs."

Harry Kroto [English: 1939–] discovered that some carbon in space is different from diamond or graphite. He then worked with Richard Smalley [American: 1943–], who was studying how small numbers of atoms cluster together. Smalley's laboratory created carbon molecules like those from space Kroto had observed. Together they recognized that the carbon atoms form a ball with 12 pentagonal faces linked by 20 hexagonal ones, like a soccer ball. Because this is the same structure as the geodesic dome invented by **Buckminster Fuller**, they named the newly recognized carbon form buckministerfullerene. Its molecule came to be called the buckyball. Soon variations were found, all with more than 60 atoms forming large balls with hexagonal and pentagonal faces, now called fullerenes, as well as long tubes with a similar structure, now called nanotubes. In the 1990s, scientists recognized that soot had always contained fullerenes, but that they had not been recognized.

Some carbon atoms form a ball with 12 pentagonal faces—just like a soccer ball.

Buckyballs and nanotubes, often modified with other elements substituted for carbon atoms or attached to them, have shown great promise in many applications, ranging from superconductors to a new form of transistor, although none is commercially available yet.

See also superconductivity.

RESOURCES

• MORE ABOUT BUCKYBALLS.

http://www.science.org.au/nova/024/024key.htm

Burbank, Luther

Horticulturist: created new plant varieties
Born: March 7, 1849, Lancaster, Massachusetts
Died: April 11, 1926, Santa Rosa, California

When Burbank was 19, he began to read the works of **Charles Darwin**, which explained the principle of natural selection. Burbank learned that by using seeds from plants with desirable characteristics it was possible to produce new plants with those same characteristics.

Luther Burbank

Burbank bought land near Lunenburg, Massachusetts, and began experimenting. He cross-bred different varieties; that is, he used the pollen from plants of one variety to pollinate flowers of plants of a different variety. The result was a hybrid variety, with some characteristics of each parent. His first success was the Burbank potato, which is larger and firmer than other potatoes. He sold the rights to the potato and used the money to move to Santa Rosa, California, where, in 1875, he established a greenhouse and experimental farm. For the next 50 years, he used various plant breeding methods to create more than 800 new kinds of plants, including more than 100 varieties of plums and 50 varieties of lilies.

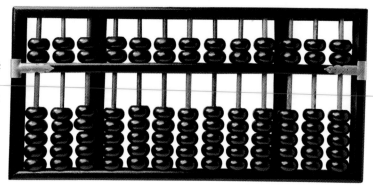
The abacus is one of the earliest counting tools.

RESOURCES

- Quackenbush, Robert. *Here a Plant, There a Plant, Everywhere a Plant, Plant: A Story of Luther Burbank*, rev. ed. Santa Rosa, CA: Luther Burbank Home & Gardens, 1995.
- LUTHER BURBANK.
  http://parks.sonoma.net/burbstory.html

Calculators

Small stones ➤ Abacus ➤ **Napier** (Napier's bones) ➤ **Oghtred** (slide rule) ➤ **Schickard** (first true calculator) ➤ **Pascal** (mechanized calculator) ➤ **Leibniz** (improvements to Pascal's calculator) ➤ **Steiger** (the Millionaire)

The first calculators were simple counters, such as small stones. They were placed on a board marked into regions to make it easy to keep track as counters were combined for addition or removed for subtraction. Making some regions worth 10

times as much as others reflected the way numbers were written, whether with special signs for 10 and 100 or with a place-value system. The counting board, with its loose counters, was improved greatly by putting the counters on wires, a device called an abacus. On an abacus it is easy to slide counters up or down or to exchange 10 counters on the 10s wire for one counter on the 100s wire.

It is easy to add or subtract on an abacus but harder to multiply or divide. John Napier [Scottish: 1550–1617] invented Napier's bones—sticks engraved with numerals that could be moved for multiplication. Napier also found a way to use exponents for multiplication and division (called logarithms when used this way). William Oughtred [English: 1574–1660] and others developed ways to use logarithms in mechanical devices. Oughtred's device, called a slide rule, remained popular for over 350 years. In Germany in 1623, Wilhelm Schickard [German: 1592-1635] made what many call the first true calculator. Schickard's machine mechanized Napier's bones. It could add, subtract, multiply, and divide.

Others made calculators based on interlocking gears. The first calculator to add and

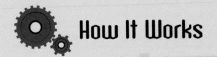

How It Works

The simplest mechanical calculator uses several gears, each with 10 times as many teeth as the one with which it meshes. The 10 teeth on the first gear represent the digits 0, 1, 2, 3, 4, 5, 6, 7, 8, 9, and, just like the numeration system the teeth on the second gear mean 10, 20, 30, 40, 50, 60, 70, 80, 90, and so forth. The gears are set so that each time one turns all the way around, it moves the next higher-numbered gear by one tooth (just like "carrying" a 1 when you add with the common pencil-and-paper method).

To add two numbers, you first move the gears to a position representing the first number. For some machines, pressing a key will set a device that will turn each gear to the appropriate position for that digit in the number when a lever is pulled to turn the gears. The number you have entered may appear as a series of digits lifted into a window by the gears. A second number is inserted with the keys. This sets the gears to turn by the amount entered. Pulling the lever a second time turns the gears by the amount of the second number, adding each amount of teeth to the amount on that gear and "carrying" whenever there is a full turn. The final position of the gears lifts the digits for the answer where they are displayed in the window.

Multiplication on such a machine is carried out by repeated addition.

Modern handheld calculators can be as powerful as some small computers.

Another popular version was marketed in 1820. In the 1880s, inventors began to produce their versions in the United States.

In 1892 Otto Steiger [German: 1870–1913] produced the first real advance over Pascal and Leibniz, a calculator called the Millionaire. It used a built-in multiplication table instead of multiplying by repeated addition. In the early 1900s, most business offices in the United States relied on mechanical calculators that also printed answers. These machines were slightly smaller than today's desktop computers.

The development of **transistors** made it possible to shrink calculators. The first "pocket" calculator was introduced in 1971. Within a few years, people stopped using slide rules and mechanical calculators. Some electric calculators became small enough to wear as watches or key

subtract using gears—basically a mechanized abacus—was developed by **Blaise Pascal** in 1642. In 1673, Gottfried Leibniz [German: 1646–1716] improved Pascal's calculator so that it could multiply and divide also. Few of the early calculator designs were actually built—some were, but largely by hand. Manufacturing methods improved during the **Industrial Revolution**. The first machine-made version of the Leibniz calculator went on sale in 1774.

rings, while others were given additional abilities that made handheld devices as powerful as small computers.

RESOURCES

- Smoothey, Marion. *Calculators* (Let's Investigate). Tarrytown, NY: Benchmark, 1995. (JUV/YA)
- History of Calculators.

  http://www.dotpoint.com/xnumber/chistory.htm

  http://www.geocities.com/SiliconValley/Horizon/1404/

Calendars

Large stones track sun's motion ➤ **Egypt** (year is 365 days) ➤ **Caesar** ("leap year") ➤ **Pope Gregory XIII** (modern calendar)

In prehistoric times it was difficult to know how to measure the length of the year. The skies hold the answer.

Early people recognized that the Sun's path changes daily. After the path has shifted as far as it can in one direction, a new year begins and the seasons repeat. Large stones (as at Stonehenge in England) or other markers kept track of the Sun's motion. In Egypt, each new year began with the rising of the brightest star, Sirius, at the exact point on the horizon where the sun sets that day. This also announced a new year and predicted the start of the annual Nile flood. Maya in Central America used the planet Venus, brighter even than Sirius, to mark the year.

Egyptians determined that one year equals 365 days—close but not exact. Measuring by the position of the Sun gives a year of 365.2422 days; measuring by Sirius (and other stars) produces 365.2654 days. In 46 B.C.E. Julius Caesar [Roman: c. 101–44 B.C.E.] instituted an extra day every

The large structures at Stonehenge in England marked the Sun's movement and are believed to be one of the world's first calendars.

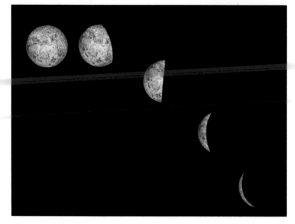

Phases of the Moon have been used in many cultures to track time.

Canals

💡 **Iraq** (canals provided irrigation and transportation) ➤ **Peru** (desert hydration) ➤ **China** (water transport) ➤ **China** (locks)

Canals—artificial waterways—are among the oldest human inventions and are still used today. Early canals bypassed rapids on the Nile (2400 B.C.E.), provided irrigation and transportation routes in Iraq (2400 B.C.E.), and linked the Mediterranean to the Red Sea (earliest version around 2000 B.C.E.). Canals made deserts flower in Peru as early as 1800 B.C.E. The Magic Canal of China linked rivers flowing north and south, opening practically the whole nation to water transport in 219 B.C.E.

Canal transportation expanded considerably after **locks** were invented in China

four years. Adding a "leap year" day makes each year average out to 365.25 days. Even more precision was added in 1582 by Pope Gregory XIII, who dropped the leap year in years ending "-00" unless the number is divisible by 400. This Gregorian calendar is still used in much of the world, adjusted by a second every few years to keep it exact.

Even before the year was recognized, people from at least 30,000 years ago marked time with the phases of the Moon. The Moon goes through one cycle of phases in about 29 days, the origin of the month. Many cultures still use a calendar combining the Moon's phases and the Sun's path. This calendar repeats after 235 lunar cycles or 19 years, which each contain the same number of days.

See also atomic clocks, clocks and watches, time.

💻📖 RESOURCES

- Maestro, Betsy C. *The Story of Clocks and Calendars: Marking a Millennium.* New York: Lothrop Lee & Shepard, 1999. (JUV/YA)
- CALENDARS THROUGH THE AGES.
  http://www.webexhibits.org/calendars/

in 983 C.E. Locks allow inland waterways to traverse hills and valleys. The 17th and 18th centuries were the "Canal Age" of transportation in Europe. In the United States, the Erie Canal, 364 miles (586 km) from Albany to Buffalo, was completed in 1825. That same year the first railroad carrying passengers and freight began making runs in England, signaling the end of canals as a major form of inland transportation.

The two major canals today are the Panama Canal across Central America, connecting the Atlantic to the Pacific, and the Suez Canal. The Suez Canal, from the Mediterranean Sea to the Red Sea, was completed in 1869 and is 105 miles (169 km) long with no locks. The Panama Canal, opened in 1914, is only 40 miles (64 km) long but cuts 7,000 miles (11,270 km) off the ocean-to-ocean distance.

RESOURCES

- Shaw, Ronald E. *Canals for a Nation: The Canal Era in the United States 1790–1860.* Lexington, KY: University Press of Kentucky, 1991.
- Spangenburg, Ray and Diane K. Moser. *The Story of America's Canals.* New York: Facts on File, 1992. (JUV/YA)
- CANALS AND INLAND WATERWAYS OF THE UNITED STATES.
  http://www.cemr.wvu.edu/venable/asa/am-rivr.htm

Carlson, Chester F.

Physicist: invented xerographic copying
Born: February 8, 1906, Seattle, Washington
Died: September 19, 1968, New York, New York

 Carlson was working in the patent department of an electronics firm in 1934. He recognized the need for mechanical **document copying** for the

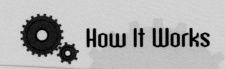 **How It Works**

A photosensitive drum is given a negative charge. Light reflected from white parts of the document to be copied removes charge where it strikes, leaving a negatively charged image of black or gray parts of the document on the drum. Positively charged ink, called toner, sticks to that image. Paper given a negative charge then lifts that image off the drum, resulting in a paper copy of the original.

many drawings and texts used in patent law. Carlson sought a method using a light-sensitive chemical to image a document and **static electricity** to transfer that image to a blank sheet of paper. After four years of experiments with this idea, he made the first copy in 1938. It then took six years for him to obtain backing for his work—more than 20 companies turned him down. Finally, he got help from the nonprofit Battelle Memorial Institute in 1944, leading to the sale of the commercial rights to a small company, later named Xerox, in 1947. It took another 11 years of development before Carlson's idea, now called xerography, was embodied in a device. Xerographic copying rapidly replaced most of the clumsy chemical methods then available.

RESOURCES

- THE NATIONAL INVENTORS HALL OF FAME.
  http://www.invent.org/book/book-text/20.html
- HISTORY OF XEROX PHOTOCOPIES AND XEROGRAPHY.
  http://inventors.about.com/science/inventors/library/inventors/blxerox.htm

Carothers, Wallace Hume

Chemist: invented nylon and neoprene
Born: April 27, 1896, Burlington, Iowa
Died: April 29, 1937, Philadelphia, Pennsylvania

 Carothers, after teaching briefly at Harvard, became head of a new division of organic chemistry research at the Du Pont chemical corporation. At Du Pont, he established by experiment the theory of how chemical units link together to form long molecules called polymers. His first application of this idea was to link together units that would imitate the structure of natural **rubber**. This led to a polymer that resists the degradation caused to natural rubber by heat, light, or chemicals. Du Pont named it neoprene and introduced it commercially in 1932. It was the first successful synthetic rubber and is still used in many applications.

Carothers hoped to create useful artificial fibers. Rayon was already in use, but although it was cheap, it was not very satisfactory in terms of wear, strength, or other properties. After experimenting with polyesters, Carothers turned to a polymer called a polyamide, from which he produced the first nylon in 1934. Du Pont introduced it in toothbrush bristles in 1938, but soon all nylon production was shunted to the needs of World War II. Since then, however, nylon has had a host of useful applications, replacing silk in clothing and wool in rugs as well as being used in solid form as a strong plastic.

 **RESOURCES**

• NATIONAL INVENTORS HALL OF FAME.

http://www.invent.org/book/book-text/21.html

Carpenters' Tools

Stonemasons (level, plumb line and square), Mallets ➤ Hammers ➤ Drills ➤ **Rome** (iron tools) ➤ Phillips screw ➤ Machine-driven drills and sanders

The earliest carpenters' tools were those invented by stonemasons: the level and plumb line used to make surfaces exactly horizontal or vertical, respectively, and the square for right angles. Mallets for driving wedges or chisels into stone were the forerunners of hammers. By 2500 B.C.E. the essential masons' tools had all been invented. Another very early tool was the drill, first used to make holes in beads and ornaments. Early drills were simple points rotated very fast, often using a bow to turn the drill.

By about 500 B.C.E. iron tools replaced stone. Roman iron tools are easily recognized as ancestors of hammers, hatchets, chisels, saws, awls, and pliers. Roman carpenters lacked screwdrivers and wrenches, however, since standardized screws and bolts were not made until the

FAMOUS FIRST

In 1841, Joseph Whitworth [English: 1803–87] developed the first standard sizes for screws and for their spirals, called "threads." Standard threads made bolts more useful, and thus standardized wrenches became common.

The basic designs of many modern tools have changed little in the past 2,000 years.

19th century. Early screws were made by hand, so each was a different size and all were expensive. Cheaper nails, also handmade, were preferred.

New tools continue to appear, such as the Phillips screw with a cross instead of a slot in its head, which requires a Phillips screwdriver. Many carpenters' tools today are machine driven, including drills and sanders. Professionals even use power-driven hammers.

Carrier, Willis

Inventor: developed air conditioning
Born: November 26, 1876, Angola, New York
Died: 1950, New York, New York

In 1902, Carrier developed a system that controls both temperature and humidity, today known as **air conditioning**. The system was installed in a Brooklyn, New York, printing plant to regulate humidity and thereby improve the quality of color printing. Carrier received a patent for his "Apparatus for Treating Air" in 1906.

Many industries began taking advantage of this new technology that improved the efficiency of machines by removing excess air moisture. Workers liked it, too; many took to eating lunch on the cool factory floor. This prompted Carrier to focus on cooling for human comfort. In 1922, he unveiled the centrifugal refrigeration machine, the first practical system for air conditioning large spaces. Soon, air conditioners were being installed in hospitals, movie theaters, and stores.

In 1928, Carrier developed the Weathermaker, the first air conditioner for homes. The Great Depression and World War II slowed acceptance of this concept. It wasn't until the late 1940s that home air conditioning started to become popular.

RESOURCES

- MORE ABOUT WILLIS CARRIER.

  http://inventors.about.com/science/
  inventors/library/weekly/aao81797.htm

  http://www.carrier.com/ghpnew/about/
  history.html

Carson, Rachel

Biologist, writer: warned of dangers of pesticides
Born: May 27, 1907, Springdale, Pennsylvania
Died: April 14, 1964, Silver Spring, Maryland

 "The more I learned about the use of pesticides, the more appalled I became," said Carson. Her book *Silent Spring* warned that widespread use of DDT and other pesticides was killing birds

Notable Quotable

For the first time... every human being is now subjected to contact with dangerous chemicals.

—**Rachel Carson**

and other animals. Some groups, particularly the chemical industry, vigorously attacked Carson and her book, but her arguments were supported by massive amounts of evidence. *Silent Spring* became

Rachel Carson

YEARBOOK: 1962

- Carson's *Silent Spring* is published.
- **Lasers** are used for the first time in eye surgery.
- *Telstar 1,* the first communications satellite, is launched.
- American Airlines introduces SABRE, the first computerized airline reservation system.

one of the most influential books of the 20th century, for it awakened the environmental movement and led to restrictions on the use of **pesticides**.

Carson grew up surrounded by cats, cows, chickens, and horses, which fostered her interest in the relationships between animals and their environment. She studied marine biology in college and, prior to *Silent Spring*, wrote three books about the sea and its organisms.

See also conservation.

💻📖 RESOURCES

- Carson, Rachel. *The Edge of the Sea.* Boston: Houghton Mifflin, 1998.
- Carson, Rachel. *Silent Spring.* Boston: Houghton Mifflin, 1994 (reprint).
- Lear, Linda. *Rachel Carson: Witness for Nature.* New York: Henry Holt, 1997.
- MORE ABOUT RACHEL CARSON.
  http://www.rachelcarson.org

Cartwright, Edmund

Inventor and clergyman: invented the power loom
Born: 1743, Marnham, England
Died: 1828, Lincoln, England

 Cartwright was an Anglican churchman who always had been attracted to invention. The **Industrial Revolution** was launched in 1733 with inventions that improved or mechanized yarn and cloth production. Cartwright observed the spinning frame used by **Richard Arkwright** in his factories and vowed to develop a loom for weaving cloth that, like Arkwright's spinning frame, would be water-powered. Although Cartwright knew nothing about looms, he spoke with local weavers, who corrected his mistakes and suggested improvements. By 1787, he had developed a water-powered loom that worked well enough for Cartwright to build his own factory. He continued to improve the power loom and eventually converted it from water to steam power. Its design has remained the basis of power looms since. Cartwright developed several other devices that contributed to the ongoing Industrial Revolution. His wool-combing machine of 1789 did the work of 20 people in preparing sheep's wool for manufacture into yarn. In 1792 he developed a machine to make rope.

Carver, George Washington

Agriculturist and chemist: developed concepts of
  crop rotation and soil renewal
Born: c. 1860, near Diamond Grove, Missouri
Died: January 5, 1943, Tuskegee, Alabama

In 1864, near the end of America's Civil War, rustlers sometimes stole slaves to sell or ransom. They captured a child slave named George along with his mother from the Missouri farm of Moses Carver. George was ransomed back, but the rustlers sold his mother.

After the war ended, George stayed with the Carver family until he was ten and took their last name. He left to work his way through school, becoming the first African-American to attend college in

Iowa. Carver earned a master's degree in agriculture in 1892. Soon, Carver started teaching at a new school for African-Americans, Tuskegee Institute in Alabama.

In the American South, former slaves often did their farming on worn-out land. Carver showed Alabama farmers ways to

George Washington Carver

Carver invented more than 150 ways to use peanuts.

renew nutrient-depleted soil. One method is by crop rotation, in which farmers plant different crops on the same patch of ground in different years. Another method is to grow certain plants, such as peanuts, soybeans, pecans, and sweet potatoes, that not only grow in poor soil but also enrich it. Since there was little demand for these soil-improving crops at that time, Carver went on to create over 300 ways to use them, from foods to plastics and paints.

YEARBOOK: 1896

- Carver begins working at Tuskegee.
- Henry Ford builds his first car.
- The first subway trains start in Budapest.
- The first inexpensive camera goes on sale for $1.
- The company that will become IBM is founded.

RESOURCES

- Carey, Charles W. *George Washington Carver* (Journey to Freedom). Chanhassen, MN: Childs World, 1999. (JUV/YA)
- Perry, John. *Unshakable Faith: Booker T. Washington & George Washington Carver.* Sisters, OR: Multinomah, 1999.
- INVENTORS HALL OF FAME.

   http://www.invent.org/book/book-text/23.html

Cathedrals

Rotated series of arches ➤ Stone ribs supporting stone domes and vaults ➤ Gothic arches, flying buttresses

A cathedral is the building that houses a bishop's church and office. In the European Middle Ages—500 to 1500 C.E.—cathedrals and other large

Cathedral of St. Peter and St. Paul, St. Petersburg, Russia

Left: *Early cathedrals featured domes formed by rotating an arch.*
Right: *Later, pointed Gothic arches and flying buttresses added new possibilities.*

churches were the most complex engineering works. Cathedrals since have followed the architectural traditions developed in those times.

From 500 to 1000 cathedrals and large churches featured domes, hemispheres formed by series of **arches** rotated on a single axis. Domes represented the heavens. Barrel vaults, rows of wide arches that form long, semicylindrical roofs, were also common. Ceilings were often made of wood, and required frequent repair or replacement.

A technological advance starting in 1050 was development of stone ribs to support stone domes and vaults, permitting much more spacious structures as well as reducing the need for repairs. Other changes include pointed (Gothic) arches, which allow higher openings for windows and doors, and flying buttresses, arching stone supports perpendicular to the exterior walls that counterbalance the outward stresses produced by heavy stone roofs.

Even with buttresses, some large cathedrals collapsed during construction or soon after. But builders learned from their disasters. Soon troops of master builders traveled from city to city, bringing with them the knowledge of how to make soaring towers and giant windows that still stand today.

RESOURCES

- ARCHITECTURE THROUGH THE AGES.

  http://library.thinkquest.org/10098/cathedrals.htm

- HISTORY OF ART.

  http://www.tam.itesm.mx/jdorante/art/gotico/igotico_004.html

Cave and Rock Art

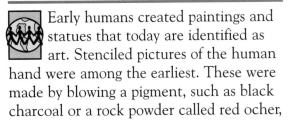

Early humans created paintings and statues that today are identified as art. Stenciled pictures of the human hand were among the earliest. These were made by blowing a pigment, such as black charcoal or a rock powder called red ocher,

Bushman painting, Kagaa Kamma, South Africa

through a tube all around an open hand flat on a surface. Small **ceramic** statues of animals or people, especially women, have been found near where people lived in huts in central Europe about 25,000 years ago.

Much of this early art is found in caves, however. About 200 caverns in southern Europe, including Lascaux, Cosquer, Chauvet, and Altamira, contain paintings, engravings, and a few sculptures. The art is 10,000 to 20,000 years old. Depictions of deer, horses, bison, and mammoths—the prey of the people living near these caves—are common, along with hand stencils.

Some who study cave art think that the paintings were intended as magic to help hunters. Many other purposes are possible, including teaching or recording important events. A famous American painting made several hundred years ago in a rock shelter shows what may be a star exploding—a supernova. Australian Aborigines still use rock paintings to help them remember the stories of earlier times.

RESOURCES

- Bahn, Paul G. and Desmond Morris. *The Cambridge Illustrated History of Prehistoric Art.* New York: Cambridge University, 1998.
- Beltran, Antonio, ed. *Cave of Altamira.* New York: Harry N. Abrams, 1999.
- Chauvet, Jean-Marie, Ellette Brunei Deschamps, Christian Hillaire, and Paul G. Bahn. *Dawn of Art: The Chauvet Cave: The Oldest Known Paintings in the World.* New York: Harry N. Abrams, 1996.
- Chippindale, Christopher and Paul S.C. Tacon, eds. *The Archaeology of Rock-Art* (New Directions in Archaeology Series). New York: Cambridge University, 1999.
- Clottes, Jean and Jean Courtin. *The Cave beneath the Sea: Paleolithic Images at Cosquer.* New York: Harry N. Abrams, 1996.

- Lauber, Patricia. *Painters of the Caves.* Washington, DC: National Geographic, 1998. (JUV/YA)

- PICTURES FROM LASCAUX.

  http://www-sor.inria.fr/pierre/lascaux/

  http://www.culture.fr/culture/arcnat/ lascaux/en/

RESOURCES

- MORE ABOUT HENRY CAVENDISH.

  http://wise.fau.edu/jordanrg/bios/Cavendish/ Cavendish_bio.htm

  http://www.mada.co.il/eng/2_1_1-22.htm

  http://web.lemoyne.edu/giunta/ Cavendish.html

Cavendish, Henry

Chemist and physicist: discovered hydrogen gas, measured Earth's density
Born: October 10, 1731, Nice, France
Died: February 24, 1810, London, England

Profoundly curious, Cavendish carried out investigations in many areas of chemistry and physics. He was the first to isolate hydrogen gas, in 1766, and showed that it is much lighter than air. He demonstrated that hydrogen is inflammable and, when burned with oxygen, produces water—proof that water is a combination of two elements rather than a fundamental element, as had been believed since the time of the ancient Greeks.

Cavendish also studied carbon dioxide, discovered by **Joseph Black** in 1756, showing that it is heavier than air and can extinguish fire.

His major achievement in physics came in 1798, when he determined Earth's density with remarkable accuracy. More than 100 years earlier, **Isaac Newton** developed his law of universal gravitation. Using a torsion balance, Cavendish provided the first experimental proof of Newton's law and concluded that Earth weighs 6,600 billion billion tons. Thus, he said, Earth's density is 5.48 times that of water. (Today, the mean density of Earth is considered to be 5.52 times that of water.)

Cayley, George

Engineer: invented the glider and founded aerodynamics
Born: December 27, 1773, Scarborough, England
Died: December 15, 1857, Brompton, England

Cayley, ten years old when balloons were invented, became interested in the challenge of flight. His ideas were modeled on soaring, rather than flapping, and his studies of birds showed that a fixed wing, if curved on its upper surface, could be successful. He experimented with kites beginning in 1804 and by 1808 developed the first gliders. In the pursuit of powered flight he invented a type of engine (the hot-air engine) and the tension spokes that make lightweight bicycle wheels possible. Although most of his efforts were aimed at developing fixed-wing aircraft and were

Gliders fly by soaring, rather than flapping.

YEARBOOK: 1853

- Human flies in heavier-than-air device.
- Corrugated steel is invented.
- First potato chip is fried.

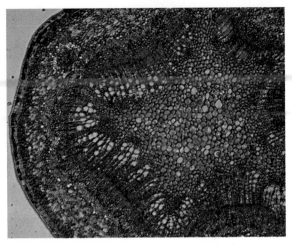

The stem of an oak tree contains many kinds of cells.

important to later airplane design, in 1843 Cayley also created the first helicopter that could fly—a small model that lifted off the ground. Ten years later, he persuaded his reluctant coachman to pilot the "Governable Parachute," the first glider to carry a human (900 feet, or 275 m).

In addition to the glider and helicopter, in 1825 Cayley invented the tractor tread and, in 1839, founded a technical school in London.

RESOURCES

- CAYLEY'S GOVERNABLE PARACHUTE.
  http://www.yorksairmuseum.freeserve.co.uk/ cayley.html

Cells

 **HOOKE** (cork cells) ➤ **VAN LEEUWENHOEK** (blood cells, sperm cells, one-celled organisms) ➤ **BROWN** (nuclei) ➤ **SCHLEIDEN/SCHWANN** (all organisms composed of cells) ➤ **VIRCHOW** (cells form cells) ➤ **(CHROMOSOMES)** ➤ **DNA/RNA** ➤**Miescher** (nuclein) ➤ **Carrel** (tissue culture)

The invention of the **microscope** led to the study of cells, which are too small to be seen with the unaided eye. In 1655, **Robert Hooke** used an early microscope to discover that cork consists of repeated units, which he called cells. In the 1670s, **Antoni van Leeuwenhoek** observed blood cells, sperm cells, and one-celled organisms.

In the 1830s, **Robert Brown** discovered that plant cells contain a nucleus (sing.); nuclei (pl.) also were observed in various animal cells. The flowing movements of a substance called protoplasm within living cells suggested that the substance is responsible for life processes. One of the most important advances in our under-standing of the meaning of life occurred in 1839, when **Matthias Schleiden** and **Theodor Schwann** proposed that all organisms are composed of one or more cells.

In 1855, **Rudolph Virchow** said that cells only arise from pre-existing cells. This

FAMOUS FIRST

All of an organism's different types of cells form from stem cells. The most basic stem cells are those involved in the early development of an embryo. In 1998, scientists at the University of Wisconsin for the first time successfully grew human embryonic stem cells in tissue culture. The technique someday may be a source of cells for transplants and for treating a variety of diseases.

Anatomy of a Cell

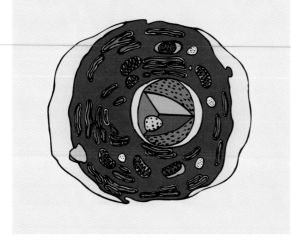

led to the discoveries of **chromosomes** and two types of cell division: mitosis, which creates two daughter cells exactly like the parent cell, and meiosis, which creates reproductive cells (eggs and sperm). Scientists also discovered that protoplasm, today called cytoplasm, contains a variety of structures, or organelles, including mitochondria (discovered in 1857), the Golgi apparatus (1898), and lysosomes (1949). Each type of structure has specific functions within the cell.

The study of cell chemistry began in 1869, when Friedrich Miescher [Swiss: 1844–1895] discovered an acid substance that he called nuclein; later work by other scientists showed that nuclein actually is a

group of compounds, today known as **DNA** and RNA.

In the early 20th century, Alexis Carrel [French-American: 1873–1944] and others developed methods of growing cells outside the body under artificial conditions—a process called **tissue culture**. This greatly expanded the study of cell movement, division, and other functions.

RESOURCES

- Rensberger, Boyce. *Life Itself: Exploring the Realm of the Living Cell.* New York: Oxford University, 1998.
- Cytology (The Study of Cells).

  http://www.rtt.ab.ca/rtt/tmills/cytology.html
  http://library.thinkquest.org/3564/

Ceramics

Middle East (first bricks from clay) ➤ **Japan** (ceramic pots) ➤ **Middle East** (potter's wheel, plaster-limestone) ➤ Concrete and cement ➤ **China** (porcelain) ➤ Chemical ceramics

Both the oldest and newest materials invented by humans are ceramics, ranging from clay animal figurines baked some 30,000 years ago to high-temperature superconductors, discovered in 1986 but still being fabricated in new forms. A ceramic is a hard, brittle material that is usually resistant to heat and water. Brick, tile, and pottery are ceramics formed when clay or similar materials are heated.

Notable Quotable

A few observations and much reasoning lead to error; many observations and a little reasoning lead to truth.

—Alexis Carre

Other inventions of that time include plaster—limestone heated and powdered that forms a hard ceramic when it dries—and fired bricks. **Concrete and cement**, harder, stronger, and more waterproof than plaster, were invented about 200 B.C.E. The hard, translucent ceramic porcelain was developed in China about 200 C.E.

Modern ceramics, made from pure chemicals instead of clay or powdered stone, include tiles on the space shuttle (designed to withstand very high temperatures), solid-state **lasers**, and materials exhibiting electromagnetic effects, such as computer-memory devices based on **magnetism**.

Pots can be shaped as they are spun on a potter's wheel.

RESOURCES

- Chavarria, Joaquim. *The Big Book of Ceramics: A Guide to the History, Materials, Equipment, and Techniques of Hand-Building, Molding, Throwing, Kiln-Firing, and Glazing.* New York: Watson-Guptill, 1994.
- MORE ABOUT CERAMICS.

    http://matse1.mse.uiuc.edu/tw/ceramics/ceramics.html

Plaster and cement harden from powdered minerals mixed with water. **Glass** is sometimes considered a ceramic.

Ceramics became widespread about 10,000 B.C.E. In the Middle East the first bricks were made from clay dried in the sun, but small clay objects were fired (baked in an oven). At that time in Japan, the earliest ceramic pots, known as Jomon ware, were being made. In the Middle East, manufacture of ceramic pots started about 7,000 B.C.E., and by about 3,500 B.C.E., Middle Eastern potters mechanized pot manufacture by shaping clay on a rotating horizontal disk, the first use of a **wheel**.

Challenger Expedition

Began: December 7, 1872
Ended: May 24, 1876

In 1870, Charles Wyville Thomson [Scottish: 1830–1882] persuaded the British government to mount an expedition to dredge organisms from deep in the world's oceans. The navy donated a medium-sized fighting ship, *H.M.S. Challenger*, from which most guns were removed and replaced with laboratories. Members of the Royal Society, a scientific organization, developed special tools for

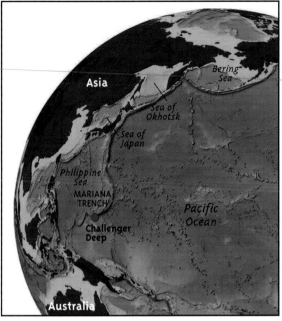

The Challanger Deep lies off the Marianas Islands.

 **RESOURCES**

• Linklater, Eric. *Voyage of the Challenger*. Garden City, NY: Doubleday, 1972.
• THE CHALLENGER SOCIETY FOR MARINE SCIENCE.

  http://www.soc.soton.ac.uk/OTHERS/CSMS/hmschall.html

Chandrasekhar, Subrahmanyan

Astrophysicist: explained how stars evolve
Born: October 19, 1910, Lahore, India (now Pakistan)
Died: August 21, 1995, Chicago, Illinois

By the 1930s scientists realized that as stars evolve their hydrogen is converted to helium and heavier elements; during the process, great amounts of energy are released. As stars age, they have less and less hydrogen. Eventually, the stars contract and become white dwarf stars. But in 1935, Chandrasekhar said that stars with a mass greater than 1.44 times the mass of the Sun (now called the

dredging and for measuring the temperature and density of lower levels of the sea. When fitted out, the *Challenger*, with a crew of about 200, set sail in December 1872 for the first round-the-world voyage to sample the depths of the seas. In addition to sails, the 226-foot (69-m) ship carried a powerful steam engine, used during scientific observations.

The *Challenger* traveled from the ice packs of the Arctic to those of the Antarctic and circumnavigated Earth over the next three-and-a-half years. Its 133 dredging runs brought to the surface 4,417 previously undiscovered organisms. Its 372 measurements of depth revealed the ocean's greatest trench off the Marianas Islands, now called the Challenger Deep, its floor 36,850 feet (11,231 m) below the surface of the Pacific Ocean. The full report of its discoveries filled 50 large volumes and was not completely in print until 1895.

Subrahmanyan Chandrasekhar

NOBEL PRIZE 1983

Chandrasekhar shared the 1983 Nobel Prize for physics with William A. Fowler [American: 1911–1995] for their studies of the changes that occur in stars. Chandrasekhar was the second family member to be so honored. His uncle, Chandrasekhara Venkata Raman [Indian: 1888–1970], received the 1930 Nobel Prize for physics for his work on the diffusion, or scattering, of light.

Chandrasekhar limit) do not follow this pattern. The more massive stars, he said, must reduce their mass, typically by becoming exploding supernovas. After such an explosion, if the remaining mass is below the limit, it will collapse into a white dwarf. But if the mass is greater, it will form a neutron star or even a black hole.

Notable Quotable

A certain modesty toward understanding nature is a precondition to the continued pursuit of science.

—**Subrahmanyan Chandrasekhar**

RESOURCES

• Srinivasan, G. *From White Dwarfs to Black Holes: The Legacy of S. Chandrasekhar.* Chicago: University of Chicago, 2000.

• Wali, Kameshwar C., ed. *Chandrasekhar: The Man Behind the Legend. Singapore:* World Scientific, 1997.

• BIOGRAPHY OF SUBRAHMANYAN CHANDRASEKHAR.

http://www.nobel.se/physics/laureates/1983/chandrasekhar-autobio.html

Charles, Jacques Alexandre

Physicist: developed law concerning expansion of gases
Born: November 12, 1746, Beaugency, France
Died: April 7, 1823, Paris, France

Charles experimented in a variety of scientific fields, including electricity and **balloons**, and invented or improved several instruments, including a goniometer for measuring angles. Around 1787, Charles found that oxygen, nitrogen, and other gases all expand by the same amount as the temperature increases, but he did not publish this discovery. In 1802, Joseph-Louis Gay-Lussac [French: 1778–1850] confirmed and expanded on the discovery and made reference in his paper to Charles' work. He formulated what came to be known as Charles' Law: If the pressure is constant, the volume occupied by a gas is directly proportional to its

Jacques Alexandre Charles

absolute temperature. Gay-Lussac also discovered another basic gas law: If the volume of a gas remains unchanged, the pressure is directly proportional to the absolute temperature.

RESOURCES

- Jacques Alexandre César Charles.
  http://onsager.bd.psu.edu/jircitano/charles.html
- Gas Laws.
  http://www.chem.uidaho.edu/honors/gas.html

Chromatography

Tswett (first development) ➤ Martin/Synge (paper chromatography)

Chromatography ("color writing") is among the most useful tools of the biochemist. Its first form was developed in 1906 by Michael Tswett [Russian-Swiss-Polish: 1872–1919] to separate plant pigments involved in **photosynthesis**. When a suspension of ground leaves is diffused through a glass cylinder filled with a fine powder, the different leaf pigments attach to the powder in different places, forming bands of color. Tswett used this method to establish that two different types of chlorophyll are involved in photosynthesis.

YEARBOOK: 1906

- Tswett invents chromatography.
- Music and voice are transmitted by **radio**.
- Freeze-drying is developed.
- August von Wasserman [German: 1866-1925] starts work on test for syphilis.

More sensitive forms of separation began with paper chromatography, first described in 1944 by Archer Martin [English: 1910–] and Richard Synge [English: 1914–1994]. Instead of a column of powder, the mixture of compounds is spread out on filter paper with a solvent and then treated with chemicals to make the bands permanent. Using this technique to separate protein fragments, scientists were able to discover the amino acid sequence of complete proteins.

Paper chromatography inspired many variations of the basic idea, including use of gases or electric currents to move suspensions through columns. Other versions use electric charge, size, or chemical affinity to separate molecules.

RESOURCES

- San Francisco's Exploratorium.
  http://www.exploratorium.edu/science_explorer/black_magic.html

Chromosomes

Beneden (fixed number of filaments per species which is halved during formation of reproductive cells) ➤ Waldeyer (terminology) ➤ Sutton (a single sperm or egg has only one member of each pair of chromosomes) ➤ Sutton/Morgan (chromosomes carry genes and pass them on) ➤ Basis for sex determination ➤ Mapping genes ➤ DNA is hereditary material ➤ Discovery of centromeres and telomeres

By the 1870s, microscopes were powerful enough to allow observation of changes that occur during **cell** division. In the nucleus of a dividing cell scientists noticed long, thin filaments. Edouard Beneden [Belgian: 1846–1910] found that each species has a fixed number of filaments, and that this number is halved during formation of reproductive cells (sperm and eggs). In 1888, Heinrich Waldeyer [German: 1836–1921] gave the filaments a name: chromosomes.

Walter Sutton [American: 1877–1916] observed that chromosomes occur in pairs in regular cells, but that a single sperm or egg has only one member of each pair. When the sperm and egg fuse during fertilization, however, the new cell contains the full number of chromosomes. In 1902, Sutton pointed out the similarity between the behavior of chromosomes and that of **Gregor Mendel's** "hereditary units." He proposed that chromosomes carry the hereditary units—today called **genes**—and pass them on from one generation to the next during reproduction. This was proven true by **Thomas Hunt Morgan**.

Meanwhile, scientists realized that chromosomes are the basis for sex determination. For example, in mammals, one particular pair of chromosomes differs in females and males. Those with two copies of the X chromosome are female, while those with one X and one Y chromosome are male.

During the remainder of the 20th century scientists began mapping the location of genes on chromosomes and determined that DNA is the hereditary material. They discovered a specialized region of a chromosome called the centromere, which is involved in division, and specialized end units called telomeres. In 1999, they discovered that the telomeres of mammalian chromosomes form loops that look like tiny lassos.

RESOURCES

- HISTORY OF GENETICS TIMELINE.
  http://www.accessexcellence.org/AE/AEPC/ WWC/1994/geneticstln.html
- INTRODUCTION TO CHROMOSOMES.
  http://gslc.genetics.utah.edu/basic/ concepts/chromosomes.html

Mouse and Human Genetic Similarities

When color-coded, the similarities between the genes of different animals, such as humans and mice, are very apparent.

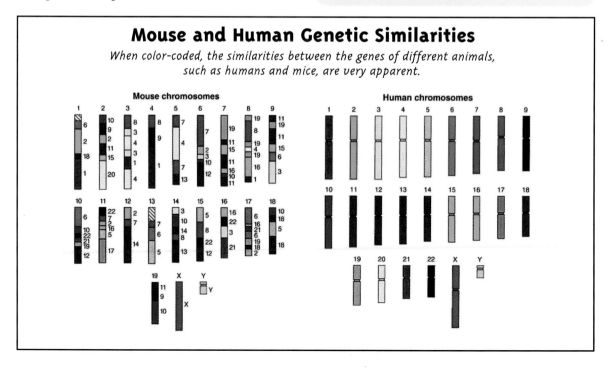

Classification of Life

ARISTOTLE (early classification) ➤ **Ray** (classification by anatomy/concept of species) ➤ **LINNAEUS** (genus to kingdom classification) ➤ **LAMARCK** (corrections to Linnaean system) ➤ **Haeckel** (addition of Protista kingdom) ➤ **Copeland** (Monera kingdom) ➤ **Whittaker** (Fungi kingdom) ➤ **Woese** (Archaea kingdom)

Scientists estimate that Earth is home to 10 million or more different kinds of organisms. Many—from giant blue whales to microscopic tuberculosis bacteria—have been described, but many more remain to be discovered and identified. To better study organisms and to understand their **evolution** and relationships to one another, a classification system, also called a taxonomy, is essential.

Aristotle was the first person known to recognize the need for classification. He

A scientific classification system provides a means of identifying relationships among organisms.

classified more than 500 species, most native to Greece and the surrounding Mediterranean Sea. He divided them in two groups, plants and animals, and further divided animals into those with red blood and those he believed, incorrectly, to have no blood (including insects and other animals with colorless blood).

Notable Quotable

Nothing is more certain to distinguish species than the criterion that true species faithfully reproduce their kind by seed.

—John Ray

No significant progress was made during the next 2,000 years. Then, in the mid-1600s, John Ray [English: 1627–1705] published systemic works on plants and several groups of animals. He classified organisms on the basis of their overall anatomy rather than on only one feature. Thus, for example, he was the first to recognize the two groups of flowering plants, monocotyledons and dicotyledons. Equally important, Ray established the concept of species—a group of individuals that are

YEARBOOK: 1686

- John Ray publishes the first volume of *Historia Plantarum [History of Plants]*, the first textbook of modern botany.
- Gottfried Wilhelm Leibniz [German: 1646–1716] publishes the first written description of integral calculus.
- **Edmond Halley** explains the cause of monsoon winds.

THE SIX KINGDOMS OF LIFE

Scientists classify all living things into one of six kingdoms.
Here is how the kingdoms are organized.

ANIMAL KINGDOM	Includes (among others) sponges, flatworms, roundworms, mollusks, segmented worms, arthropods, vertebrates, jellyfish, corals, sea anemones, echinoderms
PLANT KINGDOM	Includes (among others) ferns, mosses, ginkos, horsetails, conifers, flowering plants, liverworts, hornworts
FUNGI KINGDOM	Includes (among others) molds, mildews, blights, smuts, rusts, mushrooms, puffballs, stinkhorns, penicillia, lichens, black molds, dung fungi, yeasts, morels, truffles
PROTISTA KINGDOM	Includes (among others) yellow-green algae, golden algae, protozoa, green algae, brown algae, red algae
MONERA KINGDOM	Includes bacteria, blue-green algae
ARCHNEA KINGDOM	Certain one-celled organisms

related, nearly identical in structure, and able to interbreed.

In the 1700s, **Carolus Linnaeus** laid the foundations of the classification system used today. He grouped organisms into a series of categories, each larger than the one preceding it. Thus, similar species are grouped together in a genus, similar genera (pl. of genus) are grouped together in a family, similar families in an order, and so on up to the largest category, kingdom. As understanding of organisms grew, corrections and improvements were made to the Linnaean system. For instance, Linnaeus divided all invertebrates into insects and worms; **Jean-Baptiste Lamarck** distinguished other groups, such as mollusks and crustaceans.

Linnaeus placed all organisms in only two kingdoms: plant and animal. This sys-tem was widely accepted for more than 100 years, though in 1866 Ernst Haeckel [German: 1834–1919] proposed a third kingdom, Protista, to include all single-celled organisms. In 1938, American biologist Herbert Copeland proposed a fourth kingdom, Monera, for all bacteria. In 1969, Robert Whittaker [American: 1920–1980] proposed a fifth kingdom, Fungi.

The five-kingdom system has recently been superseded by a six-kingdom system. In the 1980s, Carl Woese [American: 1928–] demonstrated that certain one-celled organisms originally believed to be bacteria are very different, in terms of both genetics and chemistry. These organisms, many of which are adapted to life in extreme environments such as hot springs and salt ponds, are now considered a sixth kingdom, Archaea.

RESOURCES

- Margulis, Lynn and Karlene V. Schwartz. *Five Kingdoms: An Illustrated Guide to the Phyla of Life on Earth.* 3rd ed. New York: W.H. Freeman, 1997.
- MAKING SENSE OF THE SPECIES.
  http://whyfiles.org/022critters/phylogeny.html
- MORE ABOUT JOHN RAY.
  http://www.ucmp.berkeley.edu/history/ray.html

Clocks and Watches

Movement of sun and stars ➤ **Egypt** (First sundials) ➤ Water clock ➤ **China** (Toothed wheel to regulate water clock) ➤ **Italy** (Weight-driven clocks) ➤ **HUYGENS** (pendulum clock) ➤ **CURIE** (piezoelectricity) ➤ Quartz crystals ➤ Atomic clocks

Passage of **time** was originally measured by apparent movements of the Sun and stars, caused by actual movement of Earth. The ancient Egyptians divided daylight into 12 "hours" and created the first sundials to count them. By 1500 B.C.E., the sundial was joined by the water clock, in one form of which water slowly drains from a bowl marked to track the time passed since the bowl was filled. Greek inventors improved both sundials and water clocks, experimenting with elaborate forms and ways to achieve greater accuracy. The Greeks, Romans, and ancient Chinese also used water clocks to power and control various mechanical devices in order to blow whistles and open doors, for example.

About 725 C.E., Chinese monks devised an escapement to regulate water clocks. The escapement is a toothed wheel (like a gear) that moves ahead one tooth when the amount of water collected in a reservoir reaches a certain level. The movement also empties the reservoir. Each small motion, or tick, is identical so the clock is more accurate. The movement of the escapement can also be used to work with other gears to move hands on a dial or to power other devices.

Rumors of elaborate Chinese water clocks reached Italy, where large clocks with escapements and dials began to be built about 1280. Instead of using water, these clocks had a weight that slowly descended, its progress checked by an escapement. The clock face, with a single hand for the hours, was often at the top of a tower, enabling the whole town to use the clock for time and also providing a good distance for the weight to fall. Such clocks soon appeared throughout Europe. One built in Milan, Italy, in 1335, became the first to ring a bell to indicate the time.

Simple escapements are hard to control exactly, whether driven by gravity or by the power of a spring (introduced in the first portable clock, or watch, in 1502). A great advance was the pendulum clock, first built by **Galileo's** son in 1641, but made

Ancient Egyptians created the first sundials.

current produced when certain crystals are squeezed. In 1928, this idea was harnessed to run a clock regulated by a quartz crystal instead of a pendulum. Today, most watches and battery-run clocks use quartz crystals; accuracy depends on the exact shape and properties of the crystal. The most accurate clocks, however, are **atomic clocks**, used today as the world's official timekeepers.

RESOURCES

- Maestro, Betsy C. *The Story of Clocks and Calendars: Marking a Millennium*. New York: Lothrop Lee & Shepard, 1999. (JUV/YA)
- Pollard, Michael. *The Clock and How It Changed the World*. New York: Facts on File, 1995. (JUV/YA)
- NATIONAL INSTITUTE OF STANDARDS AND TECHNOLOGY. **http://physics.nist.gov/GenInt/Time/early.html**

practical by **Christiaan Huygens** starting in 1656. The pendulum, kept swinging by movement of the escapement, controls each tick with its uniform swing. Improved versions of pendulum clocks were able to keep time for several months without losing or gaining a second.

Electric clocks that are plugged into the power grid use the 60-cycle alternating current, which changes direction 60 times each second, for a timekeeper (as well as for the power for its internal mechanisms). In 1880, Pierre Curie [French: 1859–1906] discovered **piezoelectricity**, the electric

Cloning

Spemann (early experimentation) ➤ **Briggs** (tadpole cloning) ➤ **Willadsen** (mammal cloning) ➤ **Wilmut** (mammal cloning from adult cells)

A clone is an identical copy of an organism. Natural cloning is common; for example, strawberry plants send out horizontal stems that produce new plants at intervals. The new plants have exactly the same **genes** as the parent plant.

Some of the earliest artificial cloning experiments were done by Hans Spemann [German: 1869–1941]. In 1928, he performed

How It Works

A quartz crystal in a modern watch or battery-operated clock changes size in response to an electric current. The change in crystal size then generates another electric current. The combination causes the crystal to vibrate with a steady frequency, which in turn keeps the electric current in oscillation. The rest of the clock mechanism translates changes in electric current into seconds, minutes, and hours.

FAMOUS FIRST

The term "clone" was coined by geneticist J.B.S. Haldane [British: 1892–1964] in 1963.

the first nuclear transfer experiment, transferring the nucleus of a salamander embryo (undifferentiated) cell to a cell without a nucleus. The latter cell developed into a normal salamander embryo. In 1938, Spemann suggested that it might be possible to clone organisms using adult (differentiated) cells—a "fantastical experiment," he said.

In 1952, Robert Briggs [American: 1911–1983] and an associate cloned tadpoles using embryo nuclei of leopard frogs. They also tried using nuclei from adult frog cells, but the few tadpoles cloned in this manner grew abnormally.

The first to clone a mammal using embryo cells was Steen Willadsen [Danish:

1944–], who created a sheep in 1984. Two years later, scientists at the University of Wisconsin cloned a cow from embryo cells.

In 1997, it finally was announced that a mammal had been created from adult cells. Ian Wilmut [Scottish: 1944–] and associates used udder cells of a female sheep to create a lamb named Dolly, born July 5, 1996. In 1997, the same scientists created Polly, a lamb cloned from skin cells grown in a laboratory and altered to contain a human gene.

RESOURCES

- Cohen, Daniel. *Cloning.* Brookfield, CT: Millbrook, 1998. (JUV/YA)
- Kolata, Gina Bari. *Clone: The Road to Dolly, and the Path Ahead.* New York: William Morrow, 1999.
- Wilmut, Ian, Keith Campbell, and Colin Tudge. *The Second Creation: Dolly and the Age of Biological Control* . New York: Farrar, Straus & Giroux, 2000.
- CLONING GENES.
  http://esg-www.mit.edu:8001/esgbio/rdna/cloning.html
- DEVELOPMENT OF CLONING THROUGH TIME.
  http://library.thinkquest.org/24355/data/createnav.html

The first cloned mammals were sheep.

Clouds

THALES (early recognition) ➤
Howard (classification)

Water vapor rises in air, forming the high fogs we know as clouds. The water returns to Earth as rain or snow. **Thales,** at the dawn of Greek science, recognized these relationships and later Greeks worked out the details, although not always correctly. As with much ancient Greek science, speculation was valued

Cumulus clouds rise over a layer of stratus clouds.

more than experiment.

Clouds were classified in 1803 by Luke Howard [English: 1772–1864] into puffy cumulus and widespread stratus clouds 1/2 mile (1 km) high and wispy cirrus clouds about 6 miles (10 km) high. These names are combined with each other, using the prefix strato- to mean the lowest level, alto- to mean a middle level 2 to 3 miles (3 to 5 km) high, and cirro- for the highest level. Thus, a cumulus cloud can, depending on height, be a stratocumulus, altocumulus, or cirrocumulus cloud. The capacity to yield rain is indicated by the suffix -nimbus (cumulonimbus) or the prefix nimbo- (nimbostratus).

Clouds can affect air temperatures below by blocking the Sun's rays from Earth in the daytime and by trapping and reflecting back heat rising from the Earth at night.

See also weather forecasting.

FAMOUS FIRST

On November 13, 1946, **Vincent J. Schaefer** [American: 1906–1993] dropped dry ice into clouds from an airplane, causing a snowstorm over Pittsfield, Massachusetts, in the first successful attempt to influence weather.

RESOURCES

- Day, John A., Vincent J. Schaefer, and Roger Tory Peterson. *Peterson First Guide to Clouds and Weather*. Boston: Houghton-Mifflin, 1998.
- NASA's Atmospheric Infrared Sounder (AIRS) Mission.
  http://www-airs.jpl.nasa.gov/html/edu/clouds/What_are_clouds.html
- USA Today's Weather Resource.
  http://www.usatoday.com/weather/wcloudo.htm

Coal

 Marco Polo [Italian: 1254–1324], who visited China in the 13th century, reported that the Chinese burned black rocks—coal. Although unknown in Italy at that time, coal was being mined in Great Britain. By 1307, England had to restrict coal burning because of the air pollution it caused.

Coal is nearly pure carbon created from fossilized forests and swamps, pressed and heated over geological time. Deposits show the progression from damp peat through the brown, low-energy lignite to impure bituminous or soft coal. When pressure and heat are great enough, soft coal metamorphoses into anthracite (hard coal).

Coal is still burned today, primarily in power plants and factories, despite continuing problems with air pollution. In one episode in London, England, in 1952, coal smoke killed about 4,000 people.

Coal has important uses aside from heating. In 1709, Abraham Darby [English: c. 1678–1717] began production of cast iron from coke (coal with most impurities cooked out). Coke production releases a flammable gas, burned for illumination during most of the 19th century, and a thick liquid called coal tar. Coal tar became the starting point for much of the chemical industry of the 19th century. In the 20th century, petroleum replaced coal tar for many uses.

RESOURCES

- Goode, James B. *Ancient Sunshine: The Story of Coal*. Ashland, KY: Jesse Stuart Foundation, 1997.
- KENTUCKY GEOLOGICAL SURVEY.

  http://www.uky.edu/KGS/coal/webcoal/pages/coal3.htm

Coal is nearly pure carbon that has been created from fossilized forest and swamps by intense pressure and heat over millions of years.

Codes

The science of encoding messages is cryptography ("hidden writing"). The military and government have long relied on codes to keep communications secret. The ruler Julius Caesar [Roman: c. 101–44 B.C.E.] is said to have used a simple code in which one letter was substituted for another, such as C for A, D for B, and so forth. Decoding (deciphering) has determined the fate of nations. For example, British success in using predecessors of computers to decipher machine-coded German messages contributed to the German defeat in World War II. Codes are also used by businesses to prevent unauthorized peeks at information transmitted over the Internet.

Computers can encode and decode information in more complex ways than is possible by hand. Since 1976, the United States government has set standards for computer-based codes. Many computer-based coding systems are based on finding two numbers whose product is a specific number over a hundred digits long, a difficult problem for even the fastest computers.

Not all codes are secret. Coding theory applies to all methods of recording or transmitting information. Semaphore encodes messages as flag combinations (invented in 1792), telegraphers send Morse code (1838), computer programmers write instructions in code (1843), and bar codes report prices and maintain inventories (1974).

See also telegraph.

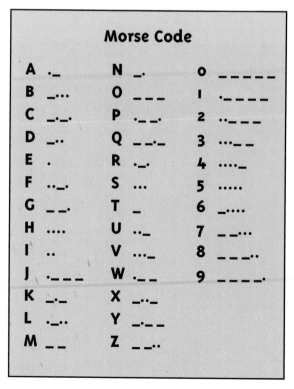

Morse Code

A	._	N	_.	0	_ _ _ _ _
B	_...	O	_ _ _	1	._ _ _ _
C	_._.	P	._ _.	2	.._ _ _
D	_..	Q	_ _._	3	..._ _
E	.	R	._.	4	...._
F	.._.	S	...	5	.....
G	_ _.	T	_	6	_....
H	....	U	.._	7	_ _...
I	..	V	..._	8	_ _ _..
J	._ _ _	W	._ _	9	_ _ _ _.
K	_._	X	_.._		
L	._..	Y	_._ _		
M	_ _	Z	_ _..		

RESOURCES

• Kahn, David. *The Codebreakers: The Comprehensive History of Secret Communication from Ancient Times to the Internet.* New York: Scribner, 1996.

• Wrixon, Fred B. *Codes, Ciphers and Other Cryptic and Clandestine Communication: 400 Ways to Send Secret Messages from Hieroglyphs to the Internet.* New York: Black Dog & Leventhal, 1998.

• CODES AND ACTIVITIES FROM THE NOVA PROGRAM "DECODING NAZI SECRETS."

  http://www.pbs.org/wgbh/nova/decoding/

Cold

Prévost (cold as lack of heat) ➤ **Fahrenheit** (developed Fahrenheit scale) ➤ **Cullen** (evaporation to lower temperature) ➤ **Joule/KELVIN** (greater cooling when gas can escape) ➤ **Cailletet** (liquefied air and other gases) ➤ **KAMERLINGH ONNES** (liquid helium)

As early as 1791, Pierre Prévost [Swiss: 1751–1839] established that cold is simply lack of **heat**. To our senses, however, cold differs from absence of heat. Specialized nerve endings in the skin, first described in 1860, respond separately to cold.

Cold is hard to produce. The temperature 0ºF on a thermometer is the coldest that Daniel Fahrenheit [Dutch: 1686–1736] could make in 1714 by mixing salt and ice. In 1756, William Cullen [Scottish: 1710–1790] suggested using evaporation to lower temperature. The gas laws also insure that a gas becomes colder and its volume decreases as pressure is lowered. Greater cooling occurs when the gas is allowed to escape freely, a result discovered in 1852 by James Prescott Joule [English: 1818–1889] and **William Thomson Baron Kelvin**. By 1878, Louis Paul Cailletet [French: 1832–1913] had used the Joule-Thomson effect to liquefy air and other gases. The coldest liquid, liquid helium, was not achieved until 1908, by **Heike Kamerlingh Onnes**.

Thomson in 1851 had used gas laws to predict that the lowest possible temperature, called absolute zero, is about -459°F (-273°C). Liquid helium is close to absolute zero. Even colder substances are produced by magnetic fields and lasers that slow motion of individual atoms. But **quantum theory** proves that no substance can be cooled all the way to absolute zero.

RESOURCES
- PROJECT SKYMATH (U.S. NATIONAL SCIENCE FOUNDATION).
  http://www.unidata.ucar.edu/staff/blynds/tmp.html
- PHYSICS 2000 (UNIVERSITY OF COLORADO PHYSICS EDUCATION PROJECT).
  http://www.colorado.edu/physics/2000/bec/temperature.html

Comets

China (earliest recorded) ➤ **Apian** (comets' tails point away from the sun) ➤ **TYCHO** (comet location) ➤ **HALLEY** (Halley's comet) ➤ **Whipple** ("dirty snowball" theory) ➤ **Oort** (comet cloud around solar system) ➤ **Kuiper** (predicted 2nd belt of comets)

Comets often appear in the sky as bright spots with long, streaky tails. The earliest record is a Chinese observation from about 2000 B.C.E. Since then, about 1,000 visible comets have been recorded—some several times on return visits.

People once thought comets signaled great changes on Earth. Scientists of the 16th century thought comets were weather phenomena, not space objects. An early clue to their real nature was the Chinese observation from 635 C.E. or earlier, rediscovered by Peter Apian [German: 1495–1552] in 1540, that comets' tails always point away from the Sun. In 1577, **Tycho Brahe** determined that a comet seen that year was much farther away than the Moon. After **Edmond Halley** studied the comet of 1682, using **Isaac Newton's** gravitational theory, he predicted in 1705 that this comet followed a regular path about the Sun and would return to Earth's vicinity in about 1758. He was correct—and we now know that Comet Halley, as it was named, has been visiting Earth every 76 years since 240 B.C.E., most recently in 1985.

The 1985 visit of Comet Halley was met with space probes from Earth, which confirmed the 1949 theory of Fred Whipple [American: 1906–] that a comet is a "dirty snowball" of frozen gases and dust. As the comet nears the Sun, the heat vaporizes outer layers, producing the giant

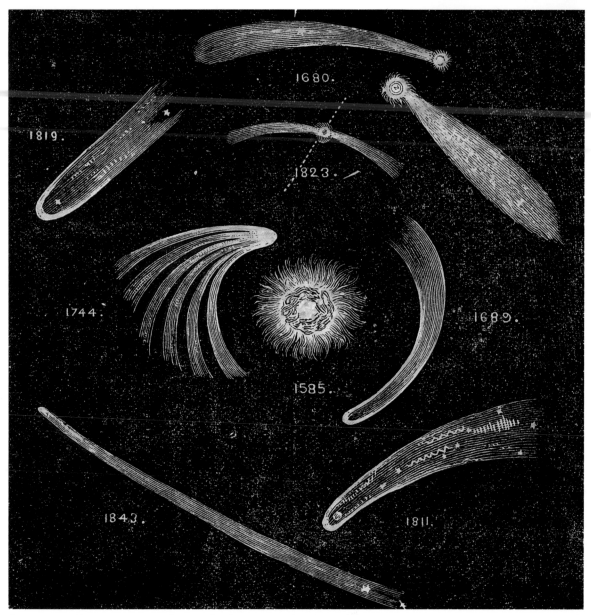

This engraving shows various types of comets that have appeared in the past.

tail, several hundred million miles long, pushed away by the solar wind as the comet approaches the Sun.

In 1950, Jan Hendrik Oort [Dutch: 1900–1992] showed that millions of comets circle the solar system in a giant cloud. The few that pass near the Sun have been pushed out of the cloud, perhaps by the gravity of a passing star. In 1951, Gerard Kuiper [Dutch-American: 1905–1973] predicted a second belt of comets orbiting just beyond Neptune. This is close enough that larger ones have since been observed.

RESOURCES

- Sagan, Carl and Ann Druyan. *Comet*. New York: Ballantine, 1997.
- Sipiera, Paul P. *Comets and Meteor Showers*. Danbury, CT: Children's, 1997. (JUV/YA)
- AMERICAN METEOR SOCIETY.
  http://comets.amsmeteors.org/
- STUDENTS FOR EXPLORATION AND DEVELOPMENT OF SPACE (SEDS).
  http://www.seds.org/billa/tnp/comets.html
- NASA's COMET OBSERVATION PAGE.
  http://encke.jpl.nasa.gov/index.html

Composites

💡 **Griffith** (glass fibers stronger than bulk glass) ➤ **Kwolek** (Kevlar)

 Many natural materials, such as bone, wood, and antler, are made from **fibers** of one material embedded in another. Such materials are called composites. Composites are often strong, lightweight, and flexible.

In 1920, A. A. Griffith [English: 1893–1963] recognized that thin fibers of glass are stronger than glass in bulk. Early glass fibers were often weakened by defects, but production problems were

eventually solved. By 1942, glass fibers embedded in plastic created fiberglass, a strong, low-density composite. Other fibers were also embedded in plastic, such as very stiff boron fibers in 1958. In 1963, fibers from a form of carbon called graphite were used. These became popular in flexible composites used for sports equipment. Kevlar, invented in 1964 by Stephanie Kwolek [American: 1923–], is five times as strong as steel and weighs less than glass, making it a popular fiber in composites used for bulletproof vests and lightweight, dentproof canoes.

RESOURCES

- COMPOSITES FABRICATORS ASSOCIATION.
  http://www.cfa-hq.org/composites.shtml
- KEVLAR.
  http://www.lbl.gov/MicroWorlds/Kevlar/

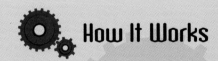 **How It Works**

In an artificial composite, fibers provide strength and stiffness, and are usually held together by a weaker low-density plastic, called the matrix. Composites can be tailored to specific needs in several ways: by choosing materials with certain properties; by using more or fewer fibers; and by varying the pattern of fibers, which can be parallel or crossed.

Compressed Air

💡 Leather bellows ➤ **Boyle** (vacuum/compressed air) ➤ Smeaton (diving bell) ➤ Pneumatic drill ➤ **Westinghouse** (air brake)

Compressed air is air under pressure greater than that of its surroundings. Blacksmiths since the 14th century have used leather bellows to compress air to make fires hotter. In the 1660s, **Robert Boyle's** air pump created vacuums and also compressed air. Boyle experimented with the effects of pressurized air on small animals.

Above: *An engraving of early diving gear*
Below: *Today, SCUBA divers carry compressed air in tanks on their back.*

In 1788, John Smeaton [English: 1724–1792] introduced a diving bell supplied with compressed air from a hand pump. Divers used compressed air from tanks in 1825 and by hose from the surface starting in 1837. The first water-powered air compressor was described in 1830. Starting in 1851, such a device supplied compressed air to underwater chambers, called caissons, used in building bridge piers.

Compressed air can transmit or store energy. The first pneumatic ("wind-filled") drill was developed in 1850 for use in building tunnels and was quickly put to use in mines as well. Today's jackhammers are still powered by compressed air, although the compressor is usually an internal combustion engine. **George Westinghouse** was inspired by pneumatic drills before inventing the air brake. At first, Westinghouse used compressed air to push a train's brake pads against its wheels, but with this method, a sudden decrease in pressure due to malfunction meant the train could not be stopped. He soon found that using air pressure to hold the brake pads away from the wheels worked better and was safer; when air pressure in the brake lines is decreased, either by a signal from the crew or by malfunction, the train will halt.

A modern air compressor

Compressed air also propels capsules through tubes. Pneumatic communication was introduced in 1853 at the London Stock Exchange and widely used in the 19th and early 20th centuries, extending hundreds of miles in some cities. It is still used by some banks to transmit money and documents at drive-in windows. Compressed air is the basis of many spray devices, including airbrushes, which spray paint, and inkjet printers. The first torpedoes, used by submarines to sink ships, were designed with compressed air motors in 1866 and some types still employ compressed air.

See also diving technology.

📺📖 RESOURCES

• Phillips, John L. *The Bends: Compressed Air in the History of Science, Diving, and Engineering.* New Haven, CT: Yale University Press, 1998.

• BRIEF HISTORY OF DIVING.
http://www.mtsinai.org/pulmonary/books/scuba/sectiona.htm

Computers

💡 **Babbage** (Analytical Engine) ➤ **Bush** (first analog computer) ➤ **Atansoff/Berry** (first computer based on binary system) ➤ **VON NEUMANN** (memory storage) ➤ **ROBERTS** (first mass-produced PC) ➤ **Jobs/Wozniak** (Apple computer)

🔌 In the 1830s, **Charles Babbage** designed the Analytical Engine, with an input device, calculating unit, memory, and other parts comparable to those found in modern computers. But it was not until the 20th century, following the development of electricity, that the dreams of people like Babbage could become reality.

In 1930, Vannevar Bush [American: 1890–1974] built the first reliable analog computer. An analog computer performs calculations based on continuously changing physical quantities, such as voltage or temperature. It's like a watch with hands that move smoothly around the face—it's easy to see when an hour has passed but impossible to determine accurately when half a second has passed.

The future lay with digital devices, which use a binary system in which there

FAMOUS FIRST

A computer is only as smart as its programs—the instructions that tell the computer what to do and how to do it. **Ada Lovelace** is often referred to as the first programmer because she wrote a list of instructions for Babbage's Analytical Engine. Today, computer programs are called "software," a term coined by John Tukey [American: 1915–2000]. He also coined the term "bit," an abbreviation of "binary digit," which refers to a unit of computer information.

are only two possibilities: an electric current is either flowing or not flowing. Modern digital computers represent all data as discrete numbers composed of binary digits (0s and 1s).

The first computer based on the binary numbering system was conceived in the late 1930s by John Atanasoff [American: 1903–1995]. Built in 1939, with the assistance of Clifford Berry [American: 1918–1963], it is known as the ABC or Atanasoff-Berry Computer. Designed to solve one type of algebraic problem, it is considered the first special-purpose electric computer.

World War II spurred computer developments. In England, highly secret Colossus computers were used to decode German

military messages. In the United States, work began on **ENIAC**. Many people consider the introduction of ENIAC in 1946 to be the start of the "computer age" in which we now live.

To this point, computers were controlled from the outside, with instructions read into the machine from punched cards or

Computers are a major part of everyday life in the 21st century.

perforated tape. In 1946, **John von Neumann** published a paper describing how instructions could be stored in a computer's memory in numerical form. The first stored program—a search for the factors of a number—was run on the Manchester Mark 1, a computer built in Manchester, England, in 1948.

Early computers were huge, filling entire rooms. The invention of **transistors** and **microprocessors** made computers smaller, faster, and more reliable. In 1960, Digital Equipment Corporation began deliveries of the first minicomputer and the first commercial computer to use a keyboard and a monitor instead of punched cards. In 1962, American Airlines launched the first computerized airline reservation system, processing a reservation in seconds rather than the 45 minutes previously required. A year later, General Motors produced the first computer-designed automobile part: the trunk lid for 1965 Cadillacs.

In 1975, a small electronics company

The invention of microprocessors (below) and transistors made computers smaller, faster, and portable.

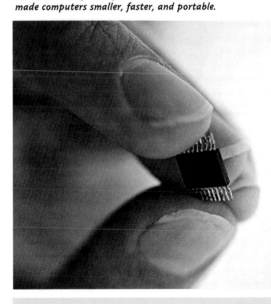

Notable Quotable

I have always taken the position that there is enough credit for everyone in the invention and development of the electronic computer.

—John Atanasoff

headed by **H. Edward Roberts** introduced the first mass-produced personal computer (PC) and the first computer that allowed other inventors to design add-on devices. Soon hobbyists were designing their own PCs. For instance, Steven Jobs [American: 1955–] and Stephen Wozniak [American: 1950–] started building their first Apple computer in a California garage. At first, software for PCs consisted mainly of games. When the first electronic spreadsheet and sophisticated word-processing programs were introduced in the late 1970s, people began to realize that PCs could be used for more serious applications.

Another trend was gathering momentum. People began linking together, or networking, computers. This led to the development of the **Internet** in the late 1960s and, more recently, the convergence of computers with telephones and televisions.

Today, the great majority of computers are desktop, notebook, or palm models. Machines no bigger than a bag of groceries are thousands of times faster than ENIAC, they can switch quickly from one stored program to another, and they are affordable for most Americans.

RESOURCES

- Greenia, Mark W. *History of Computing: An Encyclopedia of the People and Machines That Made Computer History*. CD-ROM. Lexikon Services, 2000.
- Shurkin, Joel N. *Engines of the Mind: The Evolution of the Computer from Mainframes to Microprocessor*. New York: W.W. Norton, 1996.
- KEY EVENTS IN THE HISTORY OF COMPUTING.
  http://ei.cs.vt.edu/history/50th/30.minute.show.html
- OBSOLETE COMPUTER MUSEUM.
  http://www.obsoletecomputermuseum.org/

Concrete and Cement

Rome (combined volcanic rock with clay) ➤ **Smeaton** (pozzolana cement) ➤ **Aspdin** ➤ (Portland cement; lime and clay) ➤ Reinforced concrete

Plaster, in use for the past 8,000 years, is a hard, smooth building material made from heated limestone, powdered and mixed with sand and water. It originally coated walls of sun-dried mud. Plaster, however, is not very strong and crumbles when wet.

Plaster sometimes reacts with clay to form a waterproof layer. Roman builders about 100 B.C.E. combined a volcanic rock called pozzolana with clay to produce a plaster-like material called cement that does not dissolve in water. Pozzolana cement even hardens underwater. A material in which cement binds rocks together is called concrete; concrete was very important to Roman architecture. Some Roman buildings and arches made from concrete still stand.

Concrete lost popularity after the fall of the Roman Empire, although builders continued to use some form of cement to bind together stones or bricks. After several failed efforts by others to build a lighthouse on the dangerous Eddystone Rocks near

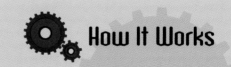

How It Works

Cement hardens because water molecules form connections, called bonds, with calcium or other minerals, not because the water evaporates and dries the mixture. Small amounts of water form strong bonds, but too much water in the mixture leaves water trapped in the cement, making it weaker.

The Pantheon of Rome is one of many huge, ancient structures built with concrete that still stands today.

Plymouth, England, in 1759, John Smeaton [English: 1724–1792] succeeded with pozzolana cement. In 1824, Joseph Aspdin [English: 1770–1855] patented a method for making what he called Portland cement from lime and clay, which with improvements by other inventors became the basis of modern cement and concrete.

Concrete resists forces that push on it, but not those that pull. A **composite** form called reinforced concrete, with iron or steel mesh or rods embedded in the concrete, is strong enough to use in building bridges and other structures that must withstand forces from several directions. Reinforced concrete was invented in 1867, but only became a major building material in the 20th century.

 **RESOURCES**

• ROMAN (AND MODERN) CONCRETE EXPLAINED.
  http://www.romanconcrete.com/

Conservation

Pinchot (1st professional forester) ➤ **Marsh** (early conservationist) ➤ **Thoreau** (suggested national forest preserves) ➤ **Audubon/Bierstadt** (wildlife artists) ➤ **Muir** (national parks) ➤ **Leopold/CARSON/Rowland** (conservationist scientists)

"Conservation means the greatest good to the greatest number for the longest time," said Gifford Pinchot [American: 1865–1946], America's first professional forester and first chief of the U.S. Forest Service. Conservation—

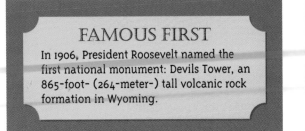

FAMOUS FIRST

In 1906, President Roosevelt named the first national monument: Devils Tower, an 865-foot- (264-meter-) tall volcanic rock formation in Wyoming.

protecting and preserving Earth's natural resources—is a comparatively new concept, with roots in the 18th century, when human populations had grown significantly and the **Industrial Revolution** had begun. As factories were built, more power was needed, which in turn created great amounts of pollution. Meanwhile, people were moving into sparsely settled lands, such as the American Midwest, cutting down vast forests and hunting animals to the verge of extinction.

By the mid-19th century in the United States, people such as George Perkins Marsh [American: 1801–1882] were calling attention to the destruction that humans were wreaking upon the Earth. The famed writer Henry David Thoreau urged the establishment of national forest preserves, and artists such as John James Audubon and Albert Bierstadt made the public aware of the

Above: *U.S. President Theodore Roosevelt is considered to be the first "conservation" president.*
Below: *Yellowstone National Park*

Timeline of U.S. Conservation and Environmental Laws

1870	Act to Prevent the Extermination of Fur-Bearing Animals in Alaska
1891	Forest Reserve Act
1900	Lacey Act
1906	Antiquities Act
1934	Taylor Grazing Act
1937	Federal Aid in Wildlife Restoration Act
1954	Watershed Protection and Flood Prevention Act
1964	Wilderness Act
1965	Solid Waste Disposal Act
1967	Air Quality Act
1969	National Environmental Policy Act; Environmental Protection Agency created
1970	Clean Air Act
1972	Water Pollution Control Act, National Marine Sanctuary Program, Coastal Zone Management Act
1973	Endangered Species Act
1975	Energy Policy and Conservation Act
1976	National Forest Management Act, Toxic Substance Control Act, Fishery Conservation and Management Act
1980	Alaska National Interest Lands Conservation Act, National Acid Precipitation Act, Comprehensive Environmental Response, Compensation and Liability Act ("Superfund")
1986	National Appliance Energy Conservation Act
1988	Ocean Dumping Ban Act
1996	Food Quality Protection Act

YEARBOOK: 1970

- The first Earth Day triggers worldwide interest in the environment.
- Retroviruses, which make DNA using an RNA template, are discovered.
- The floppy disk is introduced for storing **computer** data.
- The light-emitting diode (LED) is developed.

Yosemite and Sequoia national parks followed in 1890, thanks largely to the efforts of John Muir [Scottish-American: 1838–1914].

Interest in conservation grew throughout the 20th century, often due to public outrage following disasters, such as the near extinction of the whooping crane in 1937 and the massive 1989 oil spill in Alaskan waters from the tanker *Exxon Valdez*. Scientists such as **Aldo Leopold**, **Rachel Carson**, and **F. Sherwood Rowland** stimulated interest in saving wildlife and fighting pollution.

Notable Quotables

None of Nature's landscapes are ugly so long as they are wild.

—John Muir

The history of America has been the story of Americans seizing, using, squandering and belatedly protecting their natural heritage.

—President John F. Kennedy

The first lesson of the Alaska oil spill is that it's time for us to get serious about energy conservation.

—Washington Post editorial

beauty of the land and its wildlife. States began to pass laws for conserving wild animals and, in 1870, the U.S. Congress passed the first law to regulate hunting of fur seals in Alaska. In 1872, Yellowstone became the world's first national park.

Many conservation victories come only after long battles. Sometimes conservationists lose the battles, however. In 1872, Congress passed a law allowing companies to buy mining rights for public land for $5 an acre or less. This lead to widespread destruction of natural resources that continues to this day.

💻📖 RESOURCES

- Keene, Ann. *Earthkeepers—Observers and Protectors of Nature*. New York: Oxford University, 1994.
- Strong, Douglas. *Dreamers and Defenders—American Conservationists*. Lincoln: University of Nebraska, 1988.
- CHAMPIONS OF CONSERVATION.

  http://magazine.audubon.org/century/champion.html
- DOCUMENTARY CHRONOLOGY OF SELECTED EVENTS IN THE DEVELOPMENT OF THE AMERICAN CONSERVATION MOVEMENT, 1847-1920.

  http://memory.loc.gov/ammem/amrvhtml/cnchron1.html
- NATIONAL PARK SYSTEM TIMELINE.

  http://www.cr.nps.gov/history/timeline.htm

Conservation Laws

💡 **Lomonsov/LAVOISIER** (conservation of mass) ➤ **Mayer** (energy compared to temperature) ➤ **EINSTEIN** (energy/mass relationship) ➤ **Noether** (equivalence of symmetry)

A conservation law is a rule that the total amount of something cannot change unless there is flow into or out of the system. One of the best known is conservation of mass, first clearly stated by Mikhail Lomononsov [Russian: 1711–1765] in 1748 and independently by **Antoine-Laurent Lavoisier** in 1782. It implies that if a substance appears to lose or gain weight during a chemical change, there must be an undetected gas that

accounts for the missing mass.

Mass conservation was joined in the 1840s by conservation of energy, detailed by several scientists who carefully measured various forms of energy, ranging from motion to heat, and found that the total amount did not change during transformations from one type to another. In 1842, for example, Julius Robert Mayer [German: 1814–1878] compared the energy used in stirring a paste with the temperature rise that resulted. In 1905, **Albert Einstein** showed that energy and mass are two different aspects of the same entity. Thus, the modern conservation law is for mass and energy—in a closed system, the total amount of mass-energy cannot change.

Many other quantities are conserved. **Isaac Newton**'s third law of motion, stated in 1687, can be expressed as conservation of momentum (the product of mass and velocity). Electric charge and many other attributes of **subatomic particles** are also conserved. In 1918, Emmy Noether [German: 1881–1935] established the equivalence of symmetry, or conservation of mathematical shape, with all other conservation laws. From her point of view, any conservation law is an outgrowth of an underlying symmetry.

Copernicus, Nicolaus

Astronomer: developed heliocentric theory of the solar system
Born: Mikolaj Kopernik on February 19, 1473, Toruń, Poland
Died: May 24, 1543, Frombork, Poland

Copernicus convinced astronomers with his 1543 book *De revolutionibus orbium coelestium* [*On the Revolution of Heavenly Spheres*] that Earth and the

Nicholas Copernicus

other planets of the solar system revolve about the Sun. Although the early astronomer Aristarchus of Samos [Greek: c. 320–c. 250 B.C.E.] had also proposed this idea, he had failed to convince others. Before Copernicus, nearly everyone accepted the idea that crystal spheres centered on Earth contained the Sun, planets, and stars, all of which circled Earth inside the spheres. Copernicus had reached his conclusions as early as 1514 and circulated a short manuscript on the subject at that time. His great book was published as Copernicus was on his deathbed. His ideas were spread by later astronomers, notably **Galileo**, who found crucial evidence

supporting Copernicus, and **Johannes Kepler**, who showed that the paths of the planets are ellipses.

RESOURCES

• Gingerich, Owen. *The Eye of Heaven: Ptolemy, Copernicus, Kepler*. New York: Springer-Verlag, 1993.

Cosmic Background Radiation

HUBBLE (expansion of universe) ➤ **Gamow** (microwaves in space as result of big bang) ➤ **Dicke/Penzias/Wilson** (detection of cosmic background radiation) ➤ COBE satellite confirms

In 1929, **Edwin Hubble** showed that all parts of the universe are flying away from each other. Starting in 1948, two theories competed to explain the expansion of the universe. The steady-state theory proposed that matter is being continuously created, and the big-bang

Arno Penzias

theory postulated that creation occurred once in an event similar to an explosion. George Gamow [Russian-American, 1904–1968] established that the big bang would have permeated space with microwaves—cosmic background radiation. Robert Dicke [American: 1916–1997] planned to locate the cosmic background radiation, but as his team was building their equipment in 1965, scientists Arno Penzias [German-American, 1933–] and Robert Wilson [American: 1936–], who were trying to eliminate static from a sensitive antenna, asked Dicke to identify a pervasive signal. Dicke recognized that Penzias and Wilson had detected the cosmic background radiation, microwaves equivalent to -454°F (-270°C), confirming the big-bang theory. In the big-bang theory also, galaxies originated as slight irregularities in the original explosion.

In 1989, the United States placed the Cosmic Background Explorer (COBE) satellite in orbit, which confirmed the background radiation and its ripples.

RESOURCES

• Chown, Marcus. *Afterglow of Creation: From the Fireball to the Discovery of Cosmic Ripples.* Sausalito, CA: University Science Books, 1996.
• NASA: MICROWAVE ANISOTROPY PROBE PROJECT.
  http://map.gsfc.nasa.gov/html/cbr.html

Cosmic Rays

Hess (determined space origins) ➤ **Compton** (primary cosmic ray is a charge particle)

Early in the 20th century, physicists detected faint radiation pervading their laboratories. After evidence appeared that the radiation increases with elevation, Victor Hess [Austrian-American, 1883–1964] in 1911–1912 made ten high-altitude balloon flights that established that this radiation originates from space. Since it was present at night and during a solar eclipse, it was thought to come from "the cosmos" instead of from the Sun, so by 1925, the radiation was called "cosmic rays." The radiation Hess detected, however, originated at the top of the atmosphere. A primary cosmic ray does come from space but soon hits an atom in the atmosphere, producing a shower of secondary cosmic rays that gradually decay as they approach the surface—a few even penetrate into Earth's crust. Magnetic fields in space give primary rays twisted paths that disguise the direction of origin. Today, scientists believe that some primary cosmic rays originate with the Sun; others probably come from giant explosions of stars, called supernovas.

A primary cosmic ray is a charged particle, the nucleus of an atom, especially a hydrogen nucleus or proton, as established by Arthur Holly Compton [American: 1892–1962] in 1938. Secondary cosmic rays, however, include all kinds of particles. Each heavy particle from the collision decays into several lighter ones, which in turn, decay into even lighter ones. When physicists began to study secondary cosmic rays, they soon observed **subatomic particles** that were completely new to them. From 1932 into the 1950s, practically every new particle found was observed in secondary cosmic rays.

RESOURCES

- Clay, Roger, Bruce Dawson, and Paul Davies. *Cosmic Bullets: High Energy Particles in Astrophysics.* New York: Perseus, 1999.
- NATIONAL GEOPHYSICAL DATA CENTER.
  http://www.ngdc.noaa.gov/stp/SOLAR/ COSMIC_RAYS/cosmic.html
- GODDARD SPACE FLIGHT CENTER.
  http://www-spof.gsfc.nasa.gov/Education/ wcosray.html

Coulomb, Charles

Physicist: introduced laws of static electricity
Born: June 14, 1736, Angoulême, France
Died: August 23, 1806, Paris, France

Coulomb is best remembered today for his careful measurements and for his laws of **static electricity** and **magnetism**, but he also developed the laws of friction and of soil mechanics. He was the first investigator of properties of materials after **Galileo** and **Robert Hooke.**

Coulomb's work with the forces of electric charge and magnetism depended on a sensitive tool called the torsion balance, which he invented in 1777. A stiff fiber

suspended two masses, one of which encountered the force to be measured, causing the balance to twist. Coulomb was able to show in 1785 that static electric charges obey an inverse-square law similar to the law of gravity. Further experiments revealed that the same law applies to magnetism. The unit of electric charge, the coulomb, is named in his honor.

RESOURCES

- ELECTRONIC JOURNAL OF GEOTECHNICAL ENGINEERING.
  http://geotech.civen.okstate.edu/people/ coulomb.htm

Cousteau, Jacques-Yves

Oceanographer: invented the Aqua-Lung
Born: June 11, 1910, St.-André-de-Cubzac, France
Died: June 25, 1997, Paris, France

"The best way to observe fish is to become a fish," wrote Cousteau. As a young man he loved to put on a pair of goggles and dive into the sea. But

Jacques-Yves Cousteau

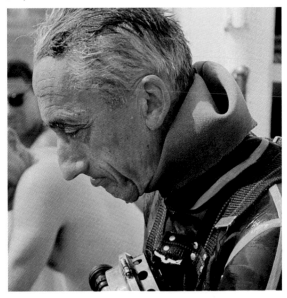

YEARBOOK: 1785

- Coulomb shows that charge obeys an inverse-square law.
- **William Herschel** discovers shape of Milky Way.
- **Henry Cavendish** determines composition of air.
- **Edmund Cartwright** invents power loom.

Cousteau was frustrated by the limitations of goggle diving. He also didn't like the heavy diving suits required for people to descend deeper into the sea. The suits were clumsy and had to have air lines connected to a ship at the surface. In 1942, Cousteau and French engineer Emile Gagnan significantly improved **diving technology** with their invention of the Aqua-Lung, or scuba (self-contained underwater breathing apparatus). The Aqua-Lung included two tanks filled with compressed air, worn on the diver's back. Hoses connected the tanks to a mouthpiece. Each time the diver inhaled, air passed from the tanks into the diver's lungs. Today's scuba equipment is very similar. Because scuba divers carry their own air supply, they can move about freely underwater.

Cousteau's second love was underwater photography. He made his first underwater movie in 1942 and invented a process for using television underwater. In 1950 he turned a former minesweeper into a research ship that he named Calypso. He sailed around the world, studying and photographing the oceans. His books and films about the sea were very popular and won many awards. In 1974, he formed the Cousteau Society, an organization dedicated to protecting the marine environment.

RESOURCES

- Markham, Lois. *Jacques-Yves Cousteau: Exploring the Wonders of the Deep*. Austin, TX: Raintree/Steck-Vaughn, 1997. (JUV/YA)
- The Cousteau Society.
  http://www.cousteausociety.org

Cranes

ARCHIMEDES (said to have used early crane) ➤
DA VINCI (improved cranes)

The crane is a construction machine used to lift heavy objects high in the air, move them horizontally, and lower them into place. Cranes, which

Tower cranes are weighted at the cab to balance heavy loads on the towers.

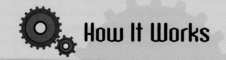

How It Works

Tower cranes, used to lift materials to the tops of skyscrapers under construction, have a heavy weight at the back of the cab to keep the tower erect. The tower has a fixed lower part and a movable upper lever called the jib. Pulley cables passing through the end of the jib lift the load and position the jib.

include derricks, may be mobile or fixed. Hoists and winches are devices similar to cranes that lift and lower loads, but do not move them horizontally.

Archimedes, who proved the laws governing the lever and other simple machines, is said to have used a crane to overturn the ships of invading Romans in 212 B.C.E. Roman engineers also used cranes, as described by Vitruvius [Roman: 1st century B.C.E.] about 25 B.C.E. One drawing from the early Roman empire shows a crane powered by four slaves walking inside a treadmill, the way a hamster turns a wheel. The same idea with only a single person inside the treadmill appears in a drawing from about 1250 C.E. **Leonardo da Vinci**, about 1499, drew improved cranes in his notebooks, but continued to indicate the use of the tread-mill as a power source.

Finally, during the **Industrial Revolution**, cranes began to be powered with **steam engines** and then later with **internal combustion engines** or even **electricity**.

Today, giant cranes are used to lift steel girders to the tops of bridges and skyscrapers. Some also lift smaller cranes to work on upper stories of buildings.

Crick, Francis

Molecular biologist: co-determined DNA structure
Born: June 8, 1916, Northampton, England

 "If you want to understand function, study structure," Crick once advised. In 1951, **James D. Watson** arrived at Cavendish Laboratory in Cambridge, England, where Crick was residing, and the two men decided to work together on determining the structure of **DNA**. They built on the work of other scientists who had studied DNA's chemical and physical characteristics and gathered data on its structure. Based on all this information, Crick and Watson in 1953 proposed that the DNA molecule is a double helix consisting of two coiled strands. Other scientists subsequently confirmed this model.

Francis Crick

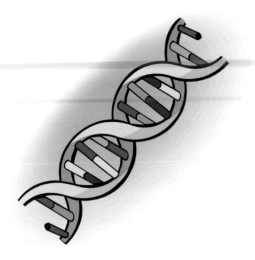

Crookes, William

Chemist: discovered thallium
Born: June 17, 1832, London, England
Died: April 4, 1919, London, England

Crookes' interest in **spectroscopy** led to his first major scientific contribution: discovery of the element thallium, announced in 1861. He then isolated the element, studied the properties of its compounds, and in 1873, determined its atomic weight using a **vacuum** chamber.

William Crookes

Crick turned his attention to **protein** synthesis and how DNA determines the sequence of amino acids in proteins. He introduced the term "codon" for a set of three adjacent DNA bases that code one amino acid. He said, correctly, that information can pass from DNA to protein, but not from protein to DNA.

In the 1960s, Crick began studying the structure and possible functions of histones, a group of proteins associated with **chromosomes**. Later in his life, his interest turned to the brain and the nature of consciousness.

See also genes.

RESOURCES

• Edelson, Edward. *Francis Crick and James Watson*. New York: Oxford University, 2000.
• Sherrow, Victoria. *Watson and Crick: Decoding the Secrets of DNA*. Woodbridge, CT: Blackbirch, 1995. (JUV/YA)
• Strathern, Paul. *Crick, Watson, and DNA*. New York: Doubleday, 1999.
• BIOGRAPHY OF FRANCIS HARRY COMPTON CRICK.

http://www.nobel.se/medicine/laureates/1962/crick-bio.html

Crookes invented the radiometer, a partial-vacuum device containing four vanes—black on one side, silver on the other—on an axle that rotates when the vanes are exposed to light. The explanation

FAMOUS FIRST

Wilhelm Rontgen discovered **X rays** using a Crookes tube.

for this was provided by George Stoney [Irish: 1826–1911] in 1876: black absorbs more radiation than silver, heating nearby air molecules, which push the black side away from the source of light.

Beginning in 1878, Crookes studied electrical discharges in partial vacuums, using a device now known as a Crookes tube. He produced glowing beams that traveled in straight lines but could be bent by a magnet, from which he concluded that they consist of charged particles. He named the beams cathode rays. Today, cathode ray tubes are used in televisions, computer monitors, and other devices.

 **RESOURCES**

- Sir William Crookes.

  http://school.discovery.com/homeworkhelp/ worldbook/atoscience/c/141380.html

Cugnot, Nicholas-Joseph

Engineer: designed first self-propelled car
Born: September 25, 1728, Void, France
Died: October 2, 1804, Paris, France

 It's difficult to define an **automobile**, but many people credit Cugnot with building the first one in 1769. Powered by a **steam engine**, it was a three-wheeled vehicle designed to pull field artillery. It carried four people and had a top speed of about 2.5 miles per hour (4 kph). Every 20 minutes or so it had to stop to build up a new head of steam in the boiler.

Cugnot built a second steam-driven car in 1770. One day, Cugnot took one of his cars out for a drive along the cobblestone streets of Paris and ran into a stone wall, producing the world's first automobile accident.

 **RESOURCES**

- History of the Automobile.

  http://www.misd.org/ sci-tech/2000/mhs/120/autohis.htm

Curie, Marie

Physicist: did pioneering work in radioactivity
Born: November 7, 1867, Warsaw, Poland
Died: July 4, 1934, Sancellemox, France

 In 1896, when **Antoine Henri Becquerel** announced that uranium emits a mysterious kind of radiation, Curie decided to study the phenomenon, which, in 1898, she named **radioactivity**. She found that the strength of radiation given off by uranium compounds is proportional to the amount of uranium present, and not affected by

Marie Curie

Nobel Prizes 1903, 1911

The 1903 Nobel Prize in physics was awarded to the Curies and Becquerel for their discovery of radioactive materials. In 1911, Marie Curie received the Nobel Prize in chemistry for her discovery of radium and polonium. She was the first person to receive two Nobel prizes in science.

disease now known to be caused by exposure to radiation.

RESOURCES

- Birch, Beverley. *Marie Curie: Courageous Pioneer in the Study of Radioactivity*. Woodbridge, CT: Blackbirch, 1996. (JUV/YA)
- Pasachoff, Naomi. *Marie Curie and the Science of Radioactivity*. New York: Oxford University, 1997. (JUV/YA)
- Strathern, Paul. *Curie and Radioactivity*. New York: Doubleday, 1999.
- Biography of Marie Sklodowska Curie.

  http://www.nobel.se/chemistry/laureates/1911/marie-curie-bio.html

temperature and other external factors. Curie discovered, however, that the compound pitchblende emits much more radiation than can be accounted for by its uranium content. She suspected that one or more unknown elements were present. In 1898, Curie and her husband, Pierre [French: 1859–1906], discovered two new radioactive elements in pitchblende, which they named radium and polonium.

Curie continued to research radioactivity and, in the 1920s, was joined in the laboratory by her daughter and son-in-law, **Irène and Frédéric Joliot-Curie**. Curie's death at age 67 was due to leukemia, a

Cycles of Nature

China (understanding of water cycle) ➤ HALLEY (proved water cycle) ➤ BLACK (carbon dioxide) ➤ Senebier (photosynthesis) ➤ Boussingault (plants use nitrogen from the soil) ➤ Winogradsky (isolated nitrifying bacteria)

Atoms of carbon, oxygen, and other materials are used over and over again in the course of nature. A carbon atom that was in a tree or dinosaur millions of years ago may be in your body today. Movement of atoms through the environment is called a cycle. There are three major cycles: water, carbon, and nitrogen.

Knowledge of these three cycles developed gradually over many centuries. The

Notable Quotables

All my life through, the new sights of Nature made me rejoice like a child.

— Marie Curie

One never notices what has been done; one can only see what remains to be done.

—Marie Curie

Marie Curie is, of all celebrated beings, the one whom fame has not corrupted.

—Albert Einstein

Chinese understood the water cycle by 500 B.C.E., but in Europe and the Americas many people considered water to be a gift from the gods. **Aristotle** suggested that river flow came from groundwater. Late in the 17th century, **Edmond Halley** demonstrated the existence of the water cycle; he calculated evaporation from the Mediterranean Sea and showed that it roughly equaled the amount of water flowing into the sea from rivers.

Recognition of the carbon and nitrogen cycles involved numerous discoveries beginning in the 18th century. Carbon dioxide first was identified in 1756 by **Joseph Black**; nitrogen was discovered in 1772 by several scientists; the absorption of carbon dioxide by plants during **photosynthesis** was shown by Jean Senebier [Swiss: 1742–1809] in 1796. In the 1850s, Jean Baptiste Joseph Dieudonné Boussingault [French: 1802–1887] demonstrated that plants require nitrogen but cannot use atmospheric nitrogen, only nitrates from the soil. In 1890, Sergei Winogradsky [Russian: 1856–1953] isolated nitrifying bacteria in the soil and demonstrated their role in the nitrogen cycle.

Study today focuses on human interactions with these cycles, such as the links between the carbon cycle and **global warming**.

📺📖 RESOURCES

- GLOBAL HYDROLOGY AND CLIMATE CENTER.
  http://www.ghcc.msfc.nasa.gov/
- THE CARBON CYCLE.
  www.gcrio.org/CONSEQUENCES/vol4no1/carbcycle.html
- UNDERSTANDING THE WATER CYCLE.
  http://unesco.org.uy/phi/libros/histwater/1history.html

Daimler, Gottlieb

Engineer: created first four-wheeled car
Born: March 17, 1834, Schorndorf, Germany
Died: March 6, 1900, Cannstatt, Germany

Daimler revolutionized the **automobile** industry in 1883 when he designed the first high-speed gasoline-driven **internal combustion engine**. This one-cylinder engine was lightweight and reliable. Earlier, working for **Nikolaus August Otto**, Daimler had helped to produce an engine that achieved 130 revolutions per minute (rpm). Daimler's new engine was much more powerful, reaching 900 rpm.

FAMOUS FIRST

In 1894, the first road race between Paris and Rouen, France, was held. Of the 102 cars that started the race, only 15 completed the course. All 15 had Daimler engines.

The new engine was first used on a boat. In 1885, Daimler and his partner, Wilhelm Maybach [German: 1846-1929], put one on a bicycle, creating what may have been the world's first motorcycle. In 1886, one of the engines was installed in a rebuilt horse carriage, creating the first four-wheeled automobile.

Daimler and Maybach then invented a four-speed gearbox and a belt drive to turn wheels. In 1889, they developed a two-cylinder engine, which was more powerful than the one-cylinder engine. They decided to sell their cars and, in 1890, founded the Daimler Motor Company, which produced the Mercedes.

RESOURCES

• Montagu, Lord, and David Burgess-Wise. *A Daimler Century: The Full History of Britain's Oldest Car Marker*. Somerset, England: J.H. Haynes, 1995.

Dalton, John

Chemist: developed the atomic theory
Born: about September 5, 1766, Eaglesfield, England
Died: July 27, 1844, Manchester, England

 As a teenager, Dalton became interested in weather, keeping a diary in which—until his death—he recorded daily observations of the atmosphere. This led him to study the different gases that make up the atmosphere. As he carried out careful measurements and experiments, he came to a conclusion that underlies the science of chemistry: the atomic theory, which he described in lectures beginning in 1803.

John Dalton

Dalton stated that all matter is composed of particles called **atoms**, that an atom is the smallest particle of an element that has the chemical characteristics of that element, and that all the atoms of an element are alike (and different from the atoms of every other element). It was later shown that atoms of an element may differ slightly in weight. Dalton's theory was confirmed by chemist William Hyde Wollaston [English: 1766–1828].

Dalton created the first table of atomic weights of elements and was the first to explain the condensation of dew. He also provided the first scientific description of colorblindness, a condition he realized he had when he found that he could not distinguish the colors of flowers.

RESOURCES

• JOHN DALTON: THE FATHER OF MODERN ATOMIC THEORY.
  http://www.sidwell.edu/apfupfu/chemistry/johndalton/
• THE PARTICLES OF MATTER AND JOHN DALTON.
  http://www.chem.ualberta.ca/courses/plambeck/p101.new/p01021.htm

Dams

Ancient Mesopotamia (wells) ➤ Jordan/Egypt (dams) ➤ Ancient Rome (concrete dams) ➤ Turbines at dams to produce electricity

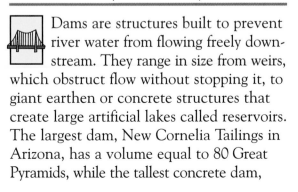 Dams are structures built to prevent river water from flowing freely downstream. They range in size from weirs, which obstruct flow without stopping it, to giant earthen or concrete structures that create large artificial lakes called reservoirs. The largest dam, New Cornelia Tailings in Arizona, has a volume equal to 80 Great Pyramids, while the tallest concrete dam,

Clockwise from top left: *Glen Canyon Dam, Arizona; Elan Valley Dam, Wales; When it was built in 1935, Hoover Dam was the largest in the world.*

Vaiont in Italy, is twice as tall as the World Trade Center in New York City.

Ancient canals in Mesopotamia, from as early as 6000 B.C.E., probably used weirs to divert water from rivers. Dams to create reservoirs in Jordan and Egypt were built about 3000 B.C.E. Early dams were generally made of clay and soil, still used for many large dams. The ancient Romans introduced concrete dams. Water wheels, turned by the flow over a dam, became increasingly popular as a source of power from Roman times through the 18th century— nearly every stream was dammed more than once along its course. Early dams often failed, sometimes producing disastrous floods. Modern dams based on scientific principles were not built until after 1860. Starting in 1882, turbines at dams have been used to generate electric power, often called hydropower. Today, more than 10 percent of the United States' electric power is generated by dams.

Dams interfere with the environment by changing rivers into lakes. They often prevent fish, notably salmon, from reaching upper reaches of rivers to reproduce. They can also prevent young fish from traveling to feeding grounds in oceans.

See also conservation, water power.

RESOURCES

- Oxlade, Christ. *Dams*. Westport, CT: Heinemann, 2000. (JUV/YA)
- UNITED STATES SOCIETY ON DAMS.
  http://www2.privatei.com/uscold/
- INTERNATIONAL RIVERS NETWORK .
  http://www.irn.org/basics/dams.shtml

Darwin, Charles

Naturalist: developed theory of natural selection
Born: February 12, 1809, Shrewsbury, England
Died: April 19, 1882, Downe, England

A scientific revolution occurred in 1859 with the publication of Darwin's *On the Origin of Species*. In this book, Darwin showed that the main force in **evolution** is a process he called "natural selection." Initially, this theory, which also was proposed by **Alfred Russel Wallace**, was controversial. Today, a slightly modified version—supported by a vast body of **fossils**, **DNA**, and other evidence—is one of the foundations of biological thought and understanding.

Darwin's life as a scientist began in late 1831, when he set sail as an unpaid naturalist aboard the *Beagle*, a British navy ship that spent the next five years traveling around the world. Wherever the ship laid anchor, Darwin gathered as many specimens as possible. He kept detailed diaries, describing the sea and sky, corals and rocks, and every kind of living creature he saw, including humans. He observed how each organism has special adaptations for obtaining food and avoiding being eaten. In South America, he found fossils of ocean life high in the Andes Mountains. He also experienced his first earthquake and saw the immense damage it caused; it was "the most awful

YEARBOOK: 1859

- The first edition of *On the Origin of Species* is published; all 1,250 copies are sold in one day.
- The world's first oil well is drilled in Titusville, Pennsylvania, striking oil on August 28.
- Construction of the Suez Canal begins.
- The **spectroscope** is introduced.

yet interesting spectacle," he wrote. In the Galapagos Islands, he was surprised that each island had similar but different kinds

Charles Darwin

of finches, mockingbirds, and tortoises.

Back in England, Darwin began developing his theory of evolution. He gathered proof from the many specimens he had collected and from other sources. For instance, he saw that there were changes in cultivated plants and domestic animals that had occurred since the start of the **Agricultural Revolution**. These resulted, he thought, from fostering and selection by humans of the traits they found most desirable. He concluded that a similar selection of traits occurs in nature. He noted that in every species there is much variety among organisms, with no two individuals exactly alike. Organisms with the traits best suited to the environment have a survival advantage; they are more likely to reproduce and pass on their traits to the next generation. Over time, he wrote, "the result of this would be the formation of a new species."

Notable Quotable

I can see no limit to the amount of change, to the beauty and complexity of the co-adaptations between all organic beings, one with another and with their physical conditions of life, which may have been affected in the long course of time through nature's power of selection, that is by the survival of the fittest.

—Charles Darwin

In addition to *On the Origin of Species*, Darwin published important works on the voyage of the *Beagle*; formation of coral atolls; classification of living and fossil barnacles; action of worms; variation among orchids, insectivorous plants, and other plants and animals; emotion in animals; and evolution of humans.

RESOURCES

- Nardo, Don. *Charles Darwin*. San Diego: Greenhaven, 2000.
- Ruse, Michael. *The Darwinian Revolution: Science Red in Tooth and Claw*. 2nd ed. Chicago: University of Chicago, 1999.
- CHRONOLOGY OF EVOLUTION.
  http://www.accessexcellence.org/AE/AEPC/WWC/1995/cron_evol.html
- FROM DARWIN TO THE HUMAN GENOME PROJECT.
  http://www.csuchico.edu/anth/CASP/Carmosino_P.html

Dating

Lyell (Earth is hundreds of thousands of years old) ➤ **Boltwood** (stages of radioactive uranium to stable lead change; measured ages of rocks) ➤ **LIBBY** (radiocarbon dating) ➤ **Bullard** (potassium-argon dating)

In the 1830s, Charles Lyell [Scottish: 1797–1875] argued that Earth is hundreds of thousands of years old (actually it is about 4 billion to 5 billion years old). Dating **rocks and minerals** and **fossils** was accomplished at that time by determining the apparent order in which rock layers formed out of sediments, looking

Trees can be dated by counting their rings.

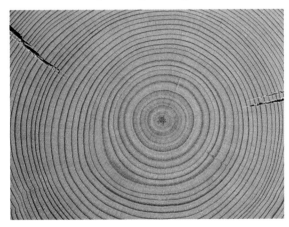

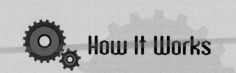

How It Works

Most dating methods use the half-life of some part of the sample. For any entity that decays at a steady rate, there exists a consistent time in which half will disappear. Based on this "half-life," mathematical methods yield the rate of change. The ratio of the end product to the original entity determines at what earlier time there existed the original only and none of the end product.

at the thickness of layers, and comparing fossils to match rocks. Two rock layers with similar fossils were assumed to have been formed at about the same date.

In 1904, Bertram Boltwood [American: 1870–1927] determined the stages through which radioactive uranium changes into stable lead. He recognized that uranium decay proceeds steadily for hundreds of thousands of years. In 1907, he suggested using this concept to measure ages of rocks. Since then, radioactive dating has been the common way to determine ages of rocks and fossils. For recent fossils, the radioactive isotope carbon-14 is used. This method, developed in 1947 by **Willard Libby**, is called radiocarbon dating. About ten years later Edward Bullard [English:1907–1980] and coworkers introduced potassium-argon dating, useful for fossils too old for carbon-14 dating.

Some specimens cannot be dated using radioactive decay. Other techniques are based on changes that take place slowly, such as alterations in form of proteins or accumulation of extra electrons as a result of cosmic ray exposure. Sometimes the

only method available is to find a layer of rock above the sample that can be dated, which then gives a minimum age.

See also geological time scale.

RESOURCES

• Bowman, Sheridan. *Radiocarbon Dating (Interpreting the Past, No. 1)*. Berkeley: University of California, 1990.
• MORE ABOUT RADIOCARBON DATING.

  http://unmuseum.mus.pa.us/radiocar.htm

  http://www.geocities.com/CapeCanaveral/Station/8985/rad.htm

Davy, Humphry

Chemist: used electricity to separate elements
Born: December 17, 1778, Penzance, England
Died: May 29, 1829, Geneva, Switzerland

Davy was a brilliant thinker who made contributions in many fields of science. In 1800, while studying the medical value of various gases, he discovered that nitrous oxide could be used as an **anesthetic**. That same year, **Alessandro Volta** announced his invention of a "pile" that used a chemical reaction to produce electric current. Davy began working with a Voltaic pile to learn about chemical effects caused by electricity— a new field of science he called electrochemistry. Davy found that when an electric current is passed through certain substances, the substances separate into elements. For example, he separated potassium from potash and sodium from common salt.

Davy proved that the green gas known as oxymuriatic acid—first isolated in 1774 by Carl Wilhelm Scheele [Swedish: 1742–1786]—is an element, which he named chlorine. He also showed that muriatic acid is a compound of hydrogen

Humphry Davy

De Broglie, Louis Victor

Physicist: recognized that all particles act like waves
Born: August 15, 1892, Dieppe, France
Died: March 19, 1987, Louveriennes, France

 De Broglie was born into the French nobility, and is often referred to by his title of Prince or Duc. In response to **Albert Einstein's** conclusion that electromagnetic waves must sometimes be treated as particles, De Broglie theorized that particles obey the equations

Louis Victor de Broglie

used to describe waves. He established the mathematical background for this in 1924. In 1926, Erwin Schrödinger [Austrian: 1887-1961] developed a form of the wave equation for the electron that became the main tool of quantum theory. Soon after, experimenters demonstrated that electrons do behave as waves.

and chlorine. These experiments disproved **Antoine Laurent Lavoisier's** theory that all acids contain oxygen.

In 1815, Davy invented the safety lamp for coal miners. Wire gauze surrounds the lamp's flame, keeping the heat away from the explosive mixture of gases in a mine. Davy did not patent the lamp, which made it easy for others to copy and use this invention.

RESOURCES

• Knight, David. *Humphry Davy, Science and Power.* New York: Cambridge University, 1998.
• Humphry Davy.
  http://www.woodrow.org/teachers/ci/1992/Davy.html

NOBEL PRIZE 1929

De Broglie received the Nobel Prize in physics for his prediction that electrons and other subatomic particles act like waves some of the time.

RESOURCES

- MORE ABOUT LOUIS VICTOR DE BROGLIE.

  http://www-groups.dcs.st-and.ac.uk/
  history/Mathematicians/Broglie.html

  http://www.nobel.se/physics/
  laureates/1929/broglie-bio.html

De Forest, Lee

Electrical engineer: developed triode vacuum tube
Born: August 26, 1873, Council Bluffs, Iowa
Died: June 30, 1961, Hollywood, California

 One of the most important developments in **radio** and **electronics** was the triode vacuum tube, invented by De Forest in 1906. The triode, which amplifies weak signals, has three locations, called electrodes, where current leaves or enters a conductor. The combined use of several triodes makes radio signals audible and also helps control volume. Triodes are also used to control other electronic signals. In most applications today, **transistors** based on the same principle are used instead of tubes.

In 1912, De Forest invented the way to use a vacuum tube to produce stronger and more regular signals from a transmitter and,

How It Works

Based on the two-electrode tube (diode) of **John Ambrose Fleming**, the triode uses a weak signal in a third electrode to modulate (control) the strong current that flows from the first electrode to the second. When the weak signal's voltage is low, current can flow freely. When the voltage is high in the weak signal, current flow is reduced. Thus the current flow is an intensified mirror image of the weak signal.

in 1923 the method used for recording sound on motion-picture film.

RESOURCES

- Wollheim, Donald. *Lee de Forest.* Chicago: Britannica Books, 1962. (YA/JUV)
- MORE ABOUT LEE DE FOREST.

  http://www.pbs.org/wgbh/aso/databank/
  entries/btfore.html

De Mestral, George

Engineer: developed Velcro
Born: 1907, Switzerland
Died: February 8, 1990, Commugny, Switzerland

 De Mestral studied the burrs that stuck to his clothing after a 1948 hunting trip. Although these plant seed cases held tightly, they could be removed with moderate force; if pushed back onto the cloth, they would stick again. De Mestral used a microscope to observe how multitudes of tiny hooks on the burrs interlocked with the loops of the fabric. He recognized that a device made with similar miniature hooks could be used to fasten clothing. By 1955, he had perfected Velcro, fabricating hooks and loops from nylon on cloth tape. The name comes from the French words for velvet [*velour*] and hooks [*crochet*]. A moderate force will separate Velcro strips, but the bond is very strong. Velcro soon became one of the world's main fastener systems, and now is made from many other materials beside nylon, depending upon the application.

RESOURCES

- MORE ABOUT DE MESTRAL.

  http://www.invent.org/book/book-text/
  mestral.html

Dentistry

Egypt/Mesopotamia (tooth filling and minor dental surgergy) ➤ **Greece/Tuscany** (tooth extraction, artificial teeth) ➤ Files for removing tooth decay ➤ Gold fillings ➤ Anesthetics ➤ Tooth X rays ➤ High-speed drill ➤ Lasers

There is evidence that the early civilizations of Egypt and Mesopotamia had access to tooth filling and other minor dental surgery about 3000 B.C.E. By the time of classical Greek and Etruscan civilizations, from 500 to 100 B.C.E., dental techniques included a special tool for extracting teeth—the forceps (rather like pliers)—and artificial teeth to replace those removed. In the Middle Ages, special files for removing tooth decay were added. By the 16th century, teeth were filled with gold after decay was removed.

Most dental procedures were extremely

Modern dentistry employs electronic and laser technology as well as a wide variety of anesthetics.

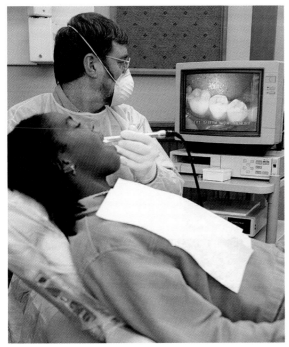

painful, so people avoided dentists until the tooth hurt more than the anticipated pain of extraction or filling. The situation improved dramatically in the 1840s, when several American dentists discovered **anesthetics**, chemicals that keep a person from feeling pain during surgical procedures. Soon after **X rays** were discovered in 1895, they began to be applied to finding hidden problems in teeth. The next big advance in painless dentistry was the high-speed drill, introduced in the 1950s. More recently, dentists have begun to use **lasers** for some dental surgery.

There are fewer dental problems today than in the recent past. Fluorides added to many water supplies since 1945 harden teeth and reduce decay. Crooked teeth are straightened early. Since 1965, teeth that are lost can be replaced with long-lasting implants.

RESOURCES

• Schissel, Marvin J. and John E. Dodes. *Healthy Teeth; A User's Manual: Everything You Need to Know to Find a Good Dentist and Take Proper Care of Your Teeth.* New York: St. Martins-Griffin, 1999.

• HISTORY OF DENTISTRY.
  http://cudental.creighton.edu/htm/history.htm
  http://www.cda.org/articles/history.htm

Dewar, James

Physicist and chemist: liquefied hydrogen and invented thermos bottle
Born: September 20, 1842, Kincardine-on-Forth, Scotland
Died: March 27, 1923, London, England

Dewar invented the vacuum flask—best known since 1904 by its commercial name of "thermos bottle"—

James Dewar

in 1872, well before he began to work with liquid gases. When French scientists liquefied nitrogen and oxygen in 1877, Dewar began to study properties of low-temperature liquid gases, especially liquid oxygen. He was able to make and store much larger quantities of liquid oxygen than other investigators because of his vacuum flask. In 1895, he became the first to liquefy hydrogen and, the following year, produced a solid form at a temperature of -434°F (-259°C). Although he was not the first, he also produced liquid helium, bringing it to a temperature just above absolute zero.

Dewar frequently collaborated with other scientists. In 1889, he worked with Frederick Abel [English: 1827–1902] to develop the "smokeless" explosive cordite, now used mainly in military rockets and pistol ammunition. His collaboration with George Liveing [English: 1827–1924] on spectroscopic studies lasted 25 years.

Dewar's wide range of interests extended from the structure of organic molecules to the production of soap bubbles—some 3 feet (1 m) in diameter.

 RESOURCES
- MORE ABOUT JAMES DEWAR.
- http://www.inventors.about.com/science/inventors/library/inventors/blthermos.htm

Diesel, Rudolf

Mechanical engineer: invented compression-ignition internal combustion engine
Born: March 18, 1858, Paris, France; German nationality
Died: September 29, 1913, English Channel

In the 1880s, Diesel began devising various types of engine, including a solar-powered air engine. He wanted to create an engine smaller than the **steam engine**, the primary power source at that time. Diesel aimed for a device that could use locally available fuels, enabling small businesses to afford a mechanical power source.

Diesel's first workable **internal combustion engine** that met his criteria was demonstrated in 1893, but he continued to improve the design. The first commercial introduction was in 1897, and Diesel started

 **How It Works**

Unlike the steam engine, where fuel burns outside the cylinder, the diesel (like the common gasoline engine) uses internal combustion. A piston heats air to a high temperature by compressing it. A fine spray of almost any kind of fuel ignites as soon as it enters the hot cylinder, which provides the power. Exhaust gases are expelled and the pattern repeats.

his own factory two years later. The efficient diesel engine became the most popular design worldwide for heavy-duty applications, especially mobile ones; modern diesel engines are usually powered by inexpensive light fuel oil.

RESOURCES

• MORE ABOUT RUDOLF DIESEL.

http://www.invent.org/book/book-text/31.html

Disease

Morgagni (disproved 4 "humors" theory) ➤ **LIND** (deficiency diseases) ➤ **Bassi** (relationship between parasites and disease) ➤ **PASTEUR/KOCH** (relationship between germs and disease) ➤ **Nicolle** (investigated spread of typhus) ➤ **Neel** (hereditary disease)

In ancient times, people in many cultures believed that gods or demons were responsible for health and illness. The Chinese believed that disease results from an imbalance between yin and yang, two life forces that flow through the body. Ancient Greeks said that disease results from a disturbance in the harmony of four bodily "humors"— blood, phlegm, yellow bile, and black bile. In medieval times, **Razi** suggested that blood causes infectious diseases.

Giovanni Battista Morgagni [Italian: 1682–1771] compared healthy and diseased organs from hundreds of cadavers. He demonstrated how symptoms of disease are associated with changes in internal organs, thereby disproving the theory of the four humors.

Agostino Bassi [Italian: 1773–1856] studied a disease of silkworms and, in 1835, announced that the disease is caused by a parasitic fungus. He theorized that other diseases also are caused by parasites. Jacob

Many infectious diseases are caused by viruses, such as these polio viruses.

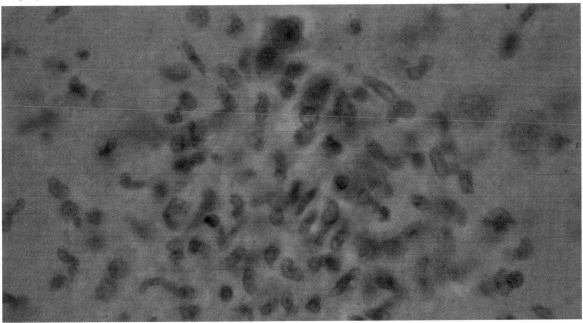

Henle [German: 1809–1885] suggested much the same in 1840, stating, "The material of contagions is not only an organic but a living one and is indeed endowed with a life of its own, which is, in relation to the diseased body, a parasitic organism." This led to the work of **Louis Pasteur** and **Robert Koch**, who independently established the germ theory of disease. Once scientists recognized the relationship between microorganisms and disease, the causes of diphtheria, tuberculosis, and other scourges were soon isolated.

Scientists also learned that disease-causing organisms are passed from one person to another in various ways. For instance, in the early 1900s, Charles Nicolle [French: 1866–1936] investigated how typhus spreads. He noticed that before entering a hospital, typhus patients frequently infected other people with the disease. But once settled in hospital beds, they did not transmit the disease. Nicolle knew that when patients were admitted to the hospital they were washed and deloused, and wondered if lice transmitted the typhus germs. He tested this theory on animals, and was able to transmit typhus to guinea pigs and monkeys. This led to efforts to change crowded, dirty living conditions in which lice are numerous.

Not all diseases result from infection. Deficiency diseases are caused by a lack of **vitamins** or other essential nutrients, as **James Lind** demonstrated in the late 1700s. Other diseases are hereditary, transferred from parent to child by **genes**; for example, in 1949 James V. Neel [American: 1915–2000] showed that sickle-cell anemia is an inherited disease. Still other diseases are caused by chemical and physical agents, such as cigarette smoke, poisons, and radiation.

See also epidemiology.

 RESOURCES

- Byers, James M. *From Hippocrates to Virchow: Reflections on Human Disease.* Chicago: ASCP, 1987.
- Cartwright, Frederick F. and Michael Biddiss. *Disease and History.* New York: Sutton, 2000.
- A Brief History of Infectious Disease.
  http://www.bayerpharma-na.com/hottopics/hc01.asp

Displays

Displays are electronic devices that create and easily change images, ranging from signs and **calculator** read-outs to **television** picture tubes. The system may be a simple pattern

Electronic displays can be seen in nearly all areas of everyday life.

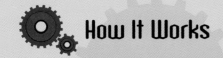

How It Works

created by light bulbs turning on and off. Other displays include cathode-ray tubes, light-emitting diodes, and liquid-crystal arrays.

The common television picture is produced by a cathode-ray tube (CRT). An electron beam lights up small dots of fluorescent materials on a screen. Magnets direct the electron beam rapidly over the entire screen while the beam is turned on and off. For color images, three different color beams work in combination to create all the screen colors we see. CRTs were used for television experiments as early as 1911. Since 1960, the CRT monitor has also been the most common display for desktop **computers**.

Light-emitting diodes (LEDs), invented by Charles A. Burrus [American: 1927–] in 1970, are essentially **transistors** that can be stimulated to glow. These are practical for simple displays on microwave ovens and digital **clocks and watches**.

Scientists at Westinghouse developed the first liquid-crystal display in 1974. Most portable computers use liquid-crystal arrays. Television sets that use liquid crystals are very flat and can hang on a wall like a painting.

Diving Technology

Diving barrel with compressed air ➤ **Siebe** (first sealed diving suit) ➤ **Haldane** (diversion of excess carbon dioxide is necessary for deep dives) ➤ **COUSTEAU/Gagnan** (scuba equipment)

Humans learn not to try to breathe underwater since they cannot obtain oxygen from water. Near the surface, a tube can bring air from above, but below three feet (1 m), it becomes impossible to breathe through the tube because hundreds of pounds of water are putting pressure on the diver's lungs.

The first successful solution, invented in 1715, enclosed the diver in a barrel that had a glass-covered porthole and openings through which arms could pass to work outside the barrel. A hose from the surface provided **compressed air**. In 1837, August Siebe [German: 1788–1872] invented the first sealed diving suit, which featured air pumped to a hard helmet attached to a rubber suit. With the diving suit, humans could descend to 120 feet (36 m), although problems developed because of the high-pressure compressed air. Air is 80 percent

Scuba equipment allows divers to swim freely.

nitrogen, and air under high pressure in the lungs causes some of that nitrogen to dissolve in the blood. As pressure decreased with a return to the surface, however, the nitrogen would come out of solution and form bubbles in the blood. Divers had to rise very slowly to prevent nitrogen bubbles from lodging in the joints and causing a permanent illness, called the "bends."

In work done during 1905–1907, J.S. Haldane [Scottish: 1860–1936] showed that carbon dioxide, accumulated in the helmet from exhalation, prevents deeper dives. By using Haldane's rules for air flow to carry off excess carbon dioxide, divers reached 200 feet (60 m) on a regular basis. Nitrogen dissolved in the blood can produce mental confusion below that depth, and so for deeper dives, other gases, such as helium, are substituted for nitrogen.

In 1943, Jacques-Yves Cousteau and French engineer Emile Gagnan developed a system that allows the diver to carry tanks of compressed air, providing freedom from the hose to the surface. His scuba (self-contained underwater breathing apparatus) equipment is now the standard for all but the deepest dives.

RESOURCES

- Dean, Anabel. *Submerge: The Story of Divers and Their Crafts.* Philadelphia: Westminster, 1976. (JUV/YA)
- Parker, Torrance R. *20,000 Jobs under the Sea: A History of Diving and Underwater Engineering.* Palos Verdes, CA: Sub-Sea Archives, 1997.
- BRIEF HISTORY OF DIVING.
- http://www.mtsinai.org/pulmonary/books/scuba/sectiona.htm
- U.S. NAVY DIVING MANUAL.
  http://www.vnh.org//DivingManual/Ch1.html

DNA

Miescher (nuclein) ➤ Levene (nucleotides) ➤ Chargaff (equal amounts of adenine/thymine and guanine/sytosine in DNA) ➤ AVERY (DNA as hereditary material), Hershey/Chase (proof of Avery's theory) ➤ Franklin (photographed DNA) ➤ WATSON/CRICK (DNA molecule is double helix)

In 1869, Friedrich Miescher [Swiss: 1844–1895] discovered an acid substance in the nuclei of pus cells and called it nuclein. Later work by other scientists showed that nuclein is present in all cells, and actually is a group of compounds, today known as DNA (deoxyribonucleic acid) and RNA (ribonucleic acid).

For seventy years after Miescher's discovery, the function of DNA was unknown. Then, in 1944, **Oswald Theodore Avery** and coworkers announced that DNA makes up **genes** and is the hereditary material of **cells**. Many scientists refused to believe this, continuing to favor the theory that proteins compose the hereditary material. Definitive proof that Avery was correct came from a famous "blender experiment" conducted by Alfred Hershey [American: 1908–1997] and his assistant Martha Chase. They grew bacteria in solution and then infected the solution with bacteriophages (viruses that attack bacteria and reproduce inside them). When all the bacteria were dead, Hershey and Chase used an ordinary kitchen blender to separate the bacteria from the viruses. They showed that the only part of the viruses that entered and reproduced within the bacteria was the DNA.

Meanwhile, efforts were underway in many labs to determine the shape of the DNA molecule. Rosalind Franklin [British: 1920–1958] used X-ray diffraction and a

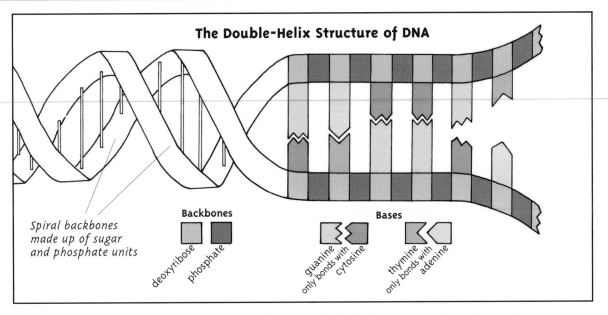

The Double-Helix Structure of DNA

Spiral backbones made up of sugar and phosphate units

Backbones

deoxyribose phosphate

Bases

guanine only bonds with cytosine

thymine only bonds with adenine

camera of her own design to photograph DNA. The photos indicated that the molecule was coiled and had a spiral form. Franklin's coworker Maurice Wilkins [British: 1916–] showed the photos to **James D. Watson**, who together with **Francis Crick** figured out that the DNA molecule is a double helix made up of two coiled strands.

Another important objective was to determine the building blocks of DNA molecules. Many scientists made contributions in this area, beginning with Phoebus Levene [Russian-American: 1869-1940]. In the late 1920s, Levene found that DNA is composed of "links" called nucleotides and that a nucleotide has three parts: a sugar unit (deoxyribose), a phosphate unit, and a nitrogen base. The development of paper chromatography in 1944 enabled Erwin Chargaff [Austrian-American: 1905–] and coworkers to study the four different bases—adenine, cytosine, guanine, and thymine—found in DNA nucleotides. In the early 1950s, they showed that the amount of adenine always equals the amount of thymine and the amount of guanine always equals the amount of cytosine. This occurs because in a DNA molecule adenine always attaches to thymine and guanine always attaches to cytosine.

-》》》》》《《《《《-

NOBEL PRIZE 1962

Watson, Crick, and Wilkins shared the Nobel Prize in physiology or medicine "for their discoveries concerning the molecular structure of nucleic acids and its significance for information transfer in living material."

-》》》》》《《《《《-

NOBEL PRIZE 1969

Hershey shared the Nobel Prize in physiology or medicine with Max Delbrück [American: 1906—1981] and Salvador Luria [American: 1912—1991] for their work on "the replication mechanism and the genetic structure of viruses."

📺📖 RESOURCES

• Lagerkvist, Ulf. *DNA Pioneers and Their Legacy.* New Haven, CT: Yale University, 1998.

• MORE ABOUT DNA.
  http://esg-www.mit.edu:8001/esgbio/ dogma/history2.html

• HISTORY OF GENETICS TIMELINE.
  http://www.accessexcellence.org/AE/ AEPC/WWC/1994/geneticstln.html

• THE BIRTH OF MOLECULAR BIOLOGY.
  http://esg-www.mit.edu:8001/esgbio/ dogma/old/dna.html

Document Copying

💡 **WATT** (early mechanical copying method) ➤ **CARLSON** (xerography) ➤ Mimeograph ➤ Carbon paper ➤ **Herschel** (blueprints) ➤ Thermography

Document copying is based on several chemical, mechanical, or light-sensitive devices used to make replicas of text or drawings. One early method, invented by **James Watt** in 1780, requires writing or drawing with special ink that transfers a copy when pressed against a sheet of paper. Schoolteachers commonly used a version

Blueprints are made by shining light through a document to create a copy on photosensitive paper.

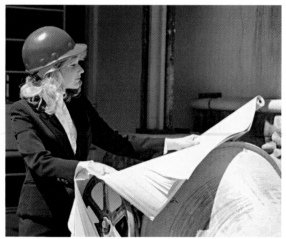

called Ditto sheets until the advent of inexpensive xerography, invented by **Chester F. Carlson**. Other copying methods also depend on making a special first document, such as a stencil in which holes in a sheet allow ink or paint to pass through to produce the copy. The mimeograph, a machine that makes multiple copies of a stencil, was invented in 1881. Carbon paper—thin paper coated with ink on one side—was invented about 1877; placed between two sheets of paper with the ink side down, it impresses a copy on the one below while the original is typed or drawn.

Blueprints are photographs made by shining a light through the document to produce a copy on photosensitive paper. The idea originated with John Herschel [English: 1792–1871] in 1840. In a true blueprint, the background is deep blue; black lines on the original become white on the print. In the 1950s, chemical methods were developed that produce dark lines against a white background. Another variation on photography is thermography, in which heat retained by black ink fixes a copy on special paper.

Some modern office copying machines use digital technology to record the original image on a chip, which then directs the copy process by causing jets of ink to be sprayed onto the page.

Domagk, Gerhard

Medical researcher: discovered first sulfonamide drug
Born: October 20, 1895, Lagow, Germany
Died: April 24, 1964, Elberfeld, Germany

 As a young man, Domagk worked in the medical corps during World War I. He saw how helpless doctors were

Gerhard Domagk

when faced with cholera, pneumonia, and other infectious diseases. After the war, Domagk completed his medical studies and began doing laboratory research. He hoped to follow in the footsteps of **Paul Ehrlich**, who had discovered a drug effective against syphilis bacteria.

In 1932, Domagk discovered that a red textile dye named Prontosil protected mice against deadly *Staphylococcus* and *Streptococcus* bacteria. Later, when his daughter was dying of a *Streptococcus* infection, Domagk gave her large injections of Prontosil and she quickly recovered. Domagk published the results of his work in 1935, revolutionizing medical treatment. Doctors were soon using Prontosil to fight many bacterial diseases.

﹥﹥﹥﹥﹥﹥﹥﹤﹤﹤﹤﹤﹤﹤

NOBEL PRIZE 1939

Domagk was awarded the Nobel Prize in physiology or medicine, but Germany's Nazi government forced him to decline the award. In 1947, following Germany's defeat in World War II, Domagk received the medal but not the money that accompanies the prize.

Prontosil was the first drug that could be used against a variety of bacteria. Other, more powerful drugs derived from Prontosil, called sulfonamides or sulfa Domagk's findings. Eventually, however, they were largely replaced by safer and more effective **antibiotics**.

See also Daniel Bovet.

 RESOURCES

• BIOGRAPHY OF GERHARD JOHANNES PAUL DOMAGK.
  http://www.nobel.se/medicine/ laureates/1939/domagk-bio.html

Domestication

About 11,000 years ago, the Agricultural Revolution resulted in animals and plants that are different from their wild relatives. The process that produces these changes is called domestication.

Domesticated cattle are smaller than their ancestors, goats have horns that are less dangerous, and domestic pigs no longer have the fearsome tusks of wild boars. People chose to hunt the most dangerous individuals and to breed the safer ones. One way to do this is to choose the animals that are most like their young—dogs that play like puppies and cats that behave like kittens. Other desirable traits are also sought, such as longer hair in sheep or more milk in cattle. Some of these gradual changes in animals are observable from bones left in the garbage heaps of early domesticators. Later, animal breeders created special breeds for special purposes, such as giant horses for pulling farm tools and long dachshunds for chasing badgers from their holes.

Plants similarly changed, with human intervention. Wild grasses, the cousins of wheat or barley, have seeds that fall to the ground as soon as they are ripe. They are not easy to pick up. Farmers harvested and later planted seeds from the few grass plants that keep the seeds longer. Eventually, grains such as maize (corn) develop, which can no longer reseed themselves because the seeds never fall, but must be removed. Similarly, grains with more seeds are preferred to those with fewer, while fruits that can be propagated from cuttings or buds, such as grapes and bananas, can stop producing their seeds completely. Pears and apples still have seeds, but domesticated varieties produce much larger fruit than their wild counterparts.

See also farming.

📺📖 RESOURCES

- Clutton-Brock, Juliet. *A Natural History of Domesticated Animals.* 2nd ed. New York: Cambridge University, 1999.
- Ryden, Hope. *Out of the Wild; The Story of Domesticated Animals.* New York: Lodestar, 1995. (JUV/YA)

Drew, Charles

Physician: developed system for storing blood plasma
Born: June 3, 1904, Washington, D.C.
Died: April 1, 1950, near Burlington, North Carolina

While he was a medical student in Montreal, Canada, Drew watched as a blood transfusion saved a man's life. This triggered Drew's interest in the preservation of blood. He conducted research on preserving blood plasma (the liquid portion of blood), which can be kept for a longer period of time than whole blood. By 1940, he had developed an efficient system for separating plasma and blood cells, storing the plasma, and transporting it. He first used this system on the battlefields of World War II, saving the lives of thousands of soldiers.

Drew also advanced the concept of blood banks—places where blood is stored for future use. During World War II, he organized the first blood bank in England and established the American Red Cross Blood Bank. His work served as a model for future blood banks and led to widespread use of blood transfusions.

Charles Drew

RESOURCES

- Shapiro, Miles. *Charles Drew, Founder of the Blood Bank.* Austin, TX: Raintree/Steck-Vaughn, 1996. (JUV/YA)
- CHARLES R. DREW.

  http://www.cdrewu.edu/about/drdrew.htm

Dwellings

Europe (caves) ➤ **Europe** (skin-covered bone frames) ➤ **Mediterranean countries** (stone houses with domed roofs) ➤ **Turkey** (brick buildings) ➤ **Mediterranean countries/India/China** (tile roofs) ➤ **Europe** (post-and-beam houses with thatched roofs) ➤ **United States** (frame houses)

During the most recent **ice ages**, some Europeans made homes in caves and rock shelters, but even then most humans lived in houses. About 15,000 years ago, for example, central Europeans made homes in mammoth-bone frameworks covered with skins. At the end of the ice age, about 11,000 years ago, people along the eastern end of the Mediterranean Sea began to build round houses about 30 feet (10 m) in diameter with stone walls, possibly with domed roofs. By 6000 B.C.E. a city in Turkey consisted of a thousand rectangular brick buildings jammed side by side—dwellers had to enter by a hole in the roof.

Various styles of houses developed. Greeks and other Mediterranean people lived in tile-roofed houses with several rooms around central courtyards, a style also used in India as early as 2300 B.C.E. and in China. In northern Europe, houses were built with posts driven into the earth; these supported wooden beams that held up thatched roofs, a style started as early as 1000 B.C.E. and still sometimes used in modified form.

In the 1830s, the frame house was invented in the United States. It is based on smaller pieces of wood and is easier and cheaper to assemble than the earlier post-and-beam house. Most homes in the United States today use frame construction, even when exterior walls are made from brick, stone, or concrete.

In Rome, starting about 200 B.C.E., many inhabitants lived in three- to five-story apartment houses. Much larger apartment houses, one with 800 rooms, were constructed by the Anasazi of southwestern North America around 1000 C.E. Large, steel-

Most houses built during colonial times in America were post-and-beam constructions.

framed apartment houses are common in cities worldwide today.

 **RESOURCES**

- Lorenz, Albert and Joy Schleh. *House: Showing How People Have Lived Throughout History with Examples Drawn from the Lives of Legendary Man and Women.* New York: Harry N. Abrams, 1998. (JUV/YA)
- Schoenauer, Norbert. *6,000 Years of Housing.* 3rd rev. ed. New York: W.W. Norton, 2000.

Dyes are used to color threads and fabrics for clothing around the world.

Dyes

💡 **Neaderthals** (dyed dead) ➤ **Phoenicians** (purple dye) ➤ **Ancient India/Egypt** (indigo) ➤ **von Hoffman** (synthetic aniline) ➤ **Perkin** (discovery of mauve) ➤ **EHRLICH** (dye use in study of disease)

 Natural plant dyes have been valued since the time of very early humans. Neandertals 80,000 years ago dyed their dead red and probably painted the bodies of the living too. About 1000 B.C.E., Phoenicians living near the Mediterranean Sea discovered how to make a purple dye from shellfish. The dye became so precious that only nobles were allowed to wear garments colored with it—and it became known as royal purple.

Indigo was a plant-derived blue dye originally popular in ancient India and Egypt. In 1826, chemists discovered that indigo heated to a high temperature yields a clear chemical named aniline (from Sanskrit for "indigo"). In 1845, synthetic aniline was produced from benzene by August Wilhelm von Hofmann [German: 1818–1892]. Benzene had just become available in large amounts from coal tar, a by-product of making coke and coal gas; it would become the basis of the chemical industry. William Henry Perkin [English: 1838-1907] in 1856 discovered a new dye, which he called mauve, while experimenting with aniline. Mauve became a great sensation, making Perkin rich, and inspiring others to seek new dyes. Hofmann, in 1858, created magenta from aniline. Other dyes were soon made from coal tar—including, in 1897, artificial indigo.

Dyes are also important in biology. Magenta stains bacteria so that they can be more easily seen. Another aniline dye, gentian violet, was used in 1884 to classify bacteria into two very different groups, based initially on whether they could be stained or not. **Paul Ehrlich** used dyes to locate parts of the immune system and to attack parasites. His successful treatment for syphilis in 1907 was based on modifying a dye by substituting arsenic for nitrogen.

Dyes remain important chemicals, often made from petroleum instead of coal tar. Many modern plastics are derived from modifications of dyes.

🖥📖 **RESOURCES**

- Delamare, François and Bernard Guineau. *Colors: The Story of Dyes and Pigments.* New York: Harry N. Abrams, 2000.